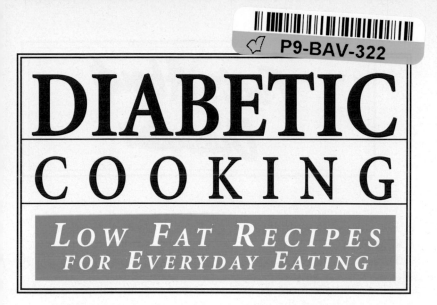

DIABETIC
COOKING

LOW FAT RECIPES FOR EVERYDAY EATING

Facts About Diabetes

Low-calorie, low-fat, low-cholesterol and low-sodium—buzzwords of the decade and for a good reason. People today are more aware than ever before of the roles that diet and exercise play in maintaining a healthful lifestyle. For people with diabetes and their families, the positive impact good nutrition and physical activity have on well-being is very familiar.

Diabetes is a disease that affects the body's ability to use glucose as a source of fuel. When glucose is improperly utilized, it can build up in the bloodstream, creating higher than normal blood sugar levels. Left unchecked, elevated blood sugar levels may lead to the development of more serious long-term complications like blindness and heart and kidney disease.

Not all cases of diabetes are alike. In fact, the disease presents itself in two very distinct forms—Type I and Type II. Development of diabetes during childhood or adolescence is typical of Type I, or juvenile-onset, diabetes. These individuals are unable to make insulin, a hormone produced by the pancreas that moves glucose from the bloodstream into the body's cells, where it is used as a source of fuel. Daily injections of insulin, coupled with a balanced meal plan, are the focus of treatment.

People who develop Type II diabetes, the more common form of the disease, are typically over the age of 40 and obese. These individuals produce insulin but the amount is insufficient to meet their needs, or their excess weight renders the hormone incapable of adequately performing its functions. Treatment includes balanced eating, moderate weight loss, exercise and, in extreme cases, oral hypoglycemic agents or insulin injections.

MAXIMIZE HEALTH, MINIMIZE COMPLICATIONS

Diabetes increases one's risk of developing high blood pressure and high blood cholesterol levels. Over time, elevated levels may progress to more serious complications, including heart and kidney disease, stroke and hypertension. In fact, research shows that individuals with diabetes are nineteen times more likely to develop kidney disease and four times more likely to suffer from heart disease or a stroke than people who do not have diabetes. While heredity plays a major role in the development of these complications, regular check-ups with your physician and registered dietitian to fine-tune treatment strategies are good ways to help minimize complications. Strategies for treatment vary among individuals, yet overall goals remain the same: achieving and maintaining near-normal blood sugar levels by balancing food intake, insulin and activity, achieving optimal blood cholesterol levels, and improving overall health through good nutrition.

BALANCE IS THE KEY

Achieving optimal nutrition often requires lifestyle changes to balance the intake of nutrients. The United States Department of Agriculture and the United States Department of Health and Human Services developed the Dietary Guidelines to simplify the basics of balanced eating and to help all individuals develop healthful eating plans. Several of the guidelines follow but were adjusted to include the revised 1994 American Diabetes Association's Nutrition Recommendations. Because recommendations are broad, work with your physician and registered dietitian to personalize the guidelines to meet your specific needs.

Eat a variety of foods.
Energy, protein, vitamins, minerals and fiber are essential for optimal health, but no one food contains them all. Including a wide range of foods in your diet and using fats and oils sparingly throughout the day are easy ways to consume all the nutrients your body needs. Carbohydrate should comprise between 45 and 55 percent of total calories, and protein should contribute between 10 and 20 percent.

Maintain a healthy weight.
Excess weight can worsen your diabetes and encourages the development of more severe complications. Research shows that shedding 10 to 20 pounds is enough to initiate positive results for obese individuals.

Combining a healthful eating plan with physical activity outlined by your health care team is the best medicine for maintaining a healthy weight.

Choose a diet low in fat, saturated fat and cholesterol. Fat has more than double the calories of an equal amount of protein or carbohydrate. Thus, diets low in fat make it easier to maintain a desirable weight and decrease the likelihood of developing high blood cholesterol levels. Limit fat to no more than 30 percent of total calories, saturated fat to no more than 10 percent of total calories and daily cholesterol to no more than 300 mg. The 30 percent of calories from fat goal applies to a total diet over time, not to a single food, serving of a recipe or meal.

Choose a diet with plenty of vegetables, fruits and grain products. Vitamins, minerals, fiber and complex carbohydrates abound in these low fat food choices. Filling up on fiber leaves less room for fat and may produce a slight decrease in blood cholesterol levels. Antioxidants such as beta carotene and the vitamins C and E may protect against heart disease, while magnesium, phosphorous and calcium are minerals that may keep blood pressure levels under control.

Use sugars in moderation. The ban on sugar has been lifted for people with diabetes but it is not altogether gone. The new guidelines for simple sugar intake are based on scientific research that indicates that carbohydrate in the form of simple sugars does not raise blood sugar levels more rapidly than any other type of carbohydrate food. What is more important is the total amount of carbohydrate consumed, not the source. However, keep in mind that since simple sugars are loaded with calories, contain no vitamins and minerals, and are linked to the development of cavities, it is still a good idea to limit your intake of simple sugars to no more than 25 percent of total carbohydrate.

Use salt and sodium in moderation. Some people with diabetes may be more sensitive to sodium than others, making them more susceptible to high blood pressure. Minimize this risk by limiting sodium intake to no more than 2,400 mg a day (about 1 teaspoon of salt) and choosing single food items with less than 400 mg of sodium and entrées with less than 800 mg of sodium per serving.

FACTS ABOUT THE FOOD

The recipes in this publication were designed with people with diabetes in mind. But all are based on the principles of sound nutrition as outlined by the Dietary Guidelines, making them perfect for the entire family. Though the recipes in this publication are not intended as a medically therapeutic program, nor as a substitute for medically approved meal plans for individuals with diabetes, they are low in calories, fat, sodium and cholesterol and will fit easily into an individualized meal plan designed by your physician, registered dietitian and you.

FACTS ABOUT THE EXCHANGES

The nutrition information that appears with each recipe was calculated by an independent nutrition consulting firm and the Dietary Exchanges are based on the Exchange Lists for Meal Planning developed by American Diabetes Association/The American Dietetic Association. Every effort has been made to check the accuracy of these numbers. However, because numerous variables account for a wide range of values in certain foods, all analyses that appear in this book should be considered approximate.

- The analysis of each recipe includes all the ingredients that are listed in that recipe, except ingredients labeled as "optional" or "for garnish."

- If a range is offered for an ingredient, the first amount given was used to calculate the nutrition information.

- If an ingredient is presented with an option ("2 cups hot cooked rice or noodles" for example), the first item listed was used to calculate the nutrition information.

- Foods shown in photographs on the same serving plate and offered as "serve with" suggestions at the end of a recipe are not included in the recipe analysis unless they are listed in the ingredient list.

- Meat should be trimmed of all visible fat since this is reflected in the nutritional analysis.

- In recipes calling for cooked rice or noodles, the analysis was based on rice or noodles that were prepared without added salt and fat.

- Most processed foods contain a significant amount of sodium and the amount of sodium is reflected in the analysis. Rinsing canned or jarred processed foods such as beans and tuna under cold running water for one minute eliminates between 40 and 60 percent of added sodium.

Sandwiches & Snacks

Add flair to midday munching with this delicious collection of sandwiches and snacks. Brown-baggers will welcome the outstanding selection of take-along treats.

Black Bean Tostadas

1 cup rinsed, drained canned black beans, mashed
2 teaspoons chili powder
Nonstick cooking spray
4 (8-inch) corn tortillas
1 cup washed, torn romaine lettuce leaves
1 cup chopped seeded tomato
½ cup chopped onion
½ cup plain nonfat yogurt
2 jalapeño peppers, seeded, finely chopped*

*Jalapeño peppers can sting and irritate the skin. Wear rubber gloves when handling peppers and do not touch eyes.

1. Combine beans and chili powder in small saucepan. Cook 5 minutes over medium heat or until heated through, stirring occasionally.

2. Spray large nonstick skillet with cooking spray. Heat over medium heat until hot. Sprinkle tortillas with water; place in skillet, one at a time. Cook 20 to 30 seconds or until hot and pliable, turning once.

3. Spread bean mixture evenly over tortillas; layer with lettuce, tomato, onion, yogurt and peppers. Garnish with cilantro, sliced tomatoes and peppers, if desired. Serve immediately.   *Makes 4 servings*

Dietary Exchanges per Serving:
1½ Starch/Bread, 1½ Vegetable

NUTRIENTS PER SERVING:

Calories	146
% calories from fat	9
Total Fat	2 g
Saturated Fat	<1 g
Cholesterol	1 mg
Sodium	466 mg
Carbohydrate	29 g
Dietary Fiber	5 g
Protein	9 g
Calcium	119 mg
Iron	2 mg
Vitamin A	129 RE
Vitamin C	18 mg

Black Bean Tostada

Meatless Sloppy Joes

2 cups thinly sliced onions
2 cups chopped green peppers
2 cloves garlic, finely chopped
2 tablespoons ketchup
1 tablespoon mustard
1 can (about 15 ounces)
    kidney beans, mashed
1 can (8 ounces) tomato sauce
1 teaspoon chili powder
    Cider vinegar
2 sandwich rolls, halved

Spray skillet with cooking spray. Add onions, peppers and garlic. Cook and stir 5 minutes over medium heat. Stir in ketchup and mustard. Add beans, sauce and chili powder. Cook 5 minutes, stirring frequently. Add ⅓ cup vinegar if dry. Serve on halves.

Makes 4 servings

Dietary Exchanges per Serving:
2 Starch/Bread, 3 Vegetable, ½ Fat

NUTRIENTS PER SERVING:

Calories	242
% calories from fat	7
Total Fat	2 g
Saturated Fat	<1 g
Cholesterol	0 mg
Sodium	994 mg
Carbohydrate	48 g
Dietary Fiber	10 g
Protein	10 g
Calcium	102 mg
Iron	3 mg
Vitamin A	158 RE
Vitamin C	113 mg

Trail Mix Truffles

⅓ cup dried apples
¼ cup dried apricots
¼ cup apple butter
2 tablespoons golden raisins
1 tablespoon reduced fat
    peanut butter
½ cup low fat granola
¼ cup graham cracker crumbs,
    divided
¼ cup mini chocolate chips

Blend fruit, apple butter, raisins and peanut butter in food processor until smooth. Stir in granola, 1 tablespoon crumbs, chips and 1 tablespoon water. Place remaining crumbs in bowl. Shape tablespoonfuls mixture into balls; roll in crumbs. Cover; refrigerate until ready to serve.

Makes 8 servings

Dietary Exchanges per Serving:
1 Starch/Bread, ½ Fruit, ½ Fat

NUTRIENTS PER SERVING:

Calories	121
% calories from fat	30
Total Fat	4 g
Saturated Fat	1 g
Cholesterol	0 mg
Sodium	14 mg
Carbohydrate	20 g
Dietary Fiber	2 g
Protein	3 g
Calcium	49 mg
Iron	1 mg
Vitamin A	30 RE
Vitamin C	1 mg

Bruschetta

1 cup thinly sliced onion
½ cup chopped seeded tomato
2 tablespoons capers
¼ teaspoon black pepper
3 cloves garlic, finely chopped
1 teaspoon olive oil
4 slices French bread
½ cup (2 ounces) shredded
    reduced fat Monterey Jack
    cheese

1. Spray large skillet with nonstick cooking spray. Heat over medium heat until hot. Add onion. Cook and stir 5 minutes. Stir in tomato, capers and pepper. Cook 3 minutes.

2. Preheat broiler. Combine garlic and oil in small bowl; brush slices with mixture. Top with onion mixture; sprinkle with cheese. Place slices on baking sheet. Broil 3 minutes or until cheese melts.

Makes 4 servings

Dietary Exchanges per Serving:
1 Starch/Bread

NUTRIENTS PER SERVING:

Calories	90
% calories from fat	20
Total Fat	2 g
Saturated Fat	<1 g
Cholesterol	0 mg
Sodium	194 mg
Carbohydrate	17 g
Dietary Fiber	<1 g
Protein	3 g
Calcium	25 mg
Iron	7 mg
Vitamin A	6 RE
Vitamin C	3 mg

California Rolls

1 cup reduced fat ricotta
    cheese
2 (11-inch) flour tortillas
1 tomato, thinly sliced
2 cups torn spinach leaves
1 cup chopped onion
½ teaspoon dried oregano
½ teaspoon dried basil
1 cup alfalfa sprouts
4 ounces sliced turkey breast

Spread cheese evenly over tortillas to within ¼ inch of edges. Layer tomato, spinach, onion, oregano, basil, alfalfa sprouts and turkey over ⅔ of each tortilla. Roll up tortillas. Wrap in plastic wrap; refrigerate 1 hour. Cut crosswise into 10 slices.

Makes 4 servings

Dietary Exchanges per Serving:
1½ Starch/Bread, 1½ Lean Meat, 1 Vegetable

NUTRIENTS PER SERVING:

Calories	209
% calories from fat	17
Total Fat	4 g
Saturated Fat	<1 g
Cholesterol	28 mg
Sodium	233 mg
Carbohydrate	28 g
Dietary Fiber	2 g
Protein	16 g
Calcium	132 mg
Iron	3 mg
Vitamin A	233 RE
Vitamin C	17 mg

South-of-the-Border Nachos

4 ounces low fat tortilla chips
Nonstick cooking spray
¾ cup chopped onion
2 jalapeño peppers, seeded, chopped*
3 cloves garlic, finely chopped
2 teaspoons chili powder
½ teaspoon ground cumin
1 boneless skinless chicken breast (about 6 ounces), cooked, chopped
1 can (14½ ounces) Mexican-style diced tomatoes, drained
1 cup (4 ounces) shredded reduced fat Monterey Jack cheese
2 tablespoons black olives, chopped

*Jalapeño peppers can sting and irritate the skin. Wear rubber gloves when handling peppers and do not touch eyes.

1. Preheat oven to 350°F. Place chips in 13×9-inch baking pan.

2. Spray large nonstick skillet with cooking spray. Heat over medium heat until hot. Add onion, peppers, garlic, chili powder and cumin. Cook 5 minutes or until vegetables are tender, stirring occasionally. Stir in chicken and tomatoes.

3. Spoon tomato mixture, cheese and olives over chips. Bake 5 minutes or until cheese melts. Serve immediately.

Makes 4 servings

Dietary Exchanges per Serving:
1 Starch/Bread, 2 Lean Meat, 1 Vegetable, ½ Fat

NUTRIENTS PER SERVING:

Calories	226
% calories from fat	26
Total Fat	7 g
Saturated Fat	2 g
Cholesterol	34 mg
Sodium	273 mg
Carbohydrate	21 g
Dietary Fiber	2 g
Protein	22 g
Calcium	377 mg
Iron	2 mg
Vitamin A	137 RE
Vitamin C	44 mg

Hummus

1 can (about 15 ounces) garbanzo beans (chick-peas), rinsed and drained
3 tablespoons lemon juice
4½ teaspoons tahini*
½ teaspoon ground cumin
¼ teaspoon salt
¼ teaspoon ground black pepper
½ cup chopped seeded tomato
⅓ cup chopped red onion
⅓ cup chopped celery
⅓ cup chopped seeded cucumber
⅓ cup chopped green or red bell pepper
2 whole pita breads

*Tahini, a thick paste made from ground sesame seeds, is available in the ethnic section of major supermarkets, Middle Eastern markets or health food stores.

1. Combine beans, lemon juice, tahini, cumin, salt and black pepper in work bowl of food processor or blender container; process until smooth. If mixture is too thick to spread, add water until desired consistency is reached.

2. Spoon bean mixture into serving bowl. Top with tomato, onion, celery, cucumber and bell pepper.

3. Preheat broiler. Split pita breads horizontally in half to form 4 rounds. Stack rounds; cut into sixths to form 24 wedges. Place wedges on baking sheet. Broil 3 minutes or until crisp.

4. Serve Hummus with warm pita bread wedges.

Makes 6 servings

Dietary Exchanges per Serving:
2 Starch/Bread, ½ Vegetable, ½ Fat

NUTRIENTS PER SERVING:
6 pita bread wedges, ½ cup Hummus

Calories	188
% calories from fat	17
Total Fat	4 g
Saturated Fat	1 g
Cholesterol	0 mg
Sodium	542 mg
Carbohydrate	33 g
Dietary Fiber	4 g
Protein	7 g
Calcium	69 mg
Iron	3 mg
Vitamin A	24 RE
Vitamin C	23 mg

Mediterranean Vegetable Sandwiches

1 small eggplant, peeled, halved, cut into ¼-inch-thick slices
Salt
1 small zucchini, halved, cut lengthwise into ¼-inch-thick slices
1 green or red bell pepper, sliced
3 tablespoons balsamic vinegar
½ teaspoon salt
½ teaspoon garlic powder
2 French bread rolls, halved

1. Place eggplant in nonaluminum colander; sprinkle eggplant with salt. Let stand 30 minutes to drain. Rinse eggplant; pat dry with paper towels.

2. Preheat broiler. Spray rack of broiler pan with nonstick cooking spray. Place vegetables on rack. Broil 4 inches from heat, 8 to 10 minutes or until vegetables are browned, turning once.

3. Combine vinegar, ½ teaspoon salt and garlic powder in medium bowl until well blended. Add vegetables; toss to coat. Divide vegetable mixture evenly between rolls. Garnish with apple slices, if desired. Serve immediately.

Makes 2 servings

Dietary Exchanges per Serving:
1½ Starch/Bread, 3 Vegetable

NUTRIENTS PER SERVING:

Calories	178
% calories from fat	10
Total Fat	2 g
Saturated Fat	<1 g
Cholesterol	0 mg
Sodium	775 mg
Carbohydrate	36 g
Dietary Fiber	1 g
Protein	5 g
Calcium	58 mg
Iron	3 mg
Vitamin A	52 RE
Vitamin C	44 mg

Health Note: Nearly 50 percent of adults with high blood pressure do not experience a reduction in blood pressure levels when the amount of sodium in their diets is reduced. Elevated levels are much more responsive to calcium-rich meals, leading many researchers to believe that good-for-your-bones calcium plays a major role in the maintenance of near-normal blood pressure levels.

Roasted Eggplant Spread

1 large eggplant
1 can (14½ ounces) diced
 tomatoes, drained
½ cup finely chopped green
 onions
½ cup chopped fresh parsley
2 tablespoons red wine
 vinegar
1 tablespoon olive oil
3 cloves garlic, finely chopped
½ teaspoon salt
½ teaspoon dried oregano
 leaves
2 pita breads

1. Preheat oven to 375°F.

2. Place eggplant on baking sheet. Bake 1 hour or until tender, turning occasionally. Remove eggplant from oven. Let stand 10 minutes or until cool enough to handle.

3. Cut eggplant lengthwise in half; remove pulp. Place pulp in medium bowl; mash with fork until smooth. Add tomatoes, onions, parsley, vinegar, oil, garlic, salt and oregano; blend well. Cover eggplant mixture; refrigerate 2 hours.

4. Preheat broiler. Split pita breads horizontally in half to form 4 rounds. Stack rounds; cut into sixths to form

24 wedges. Place wedges on baking sheet. Broil 3 minutes or until crisp.

5. Serve eggplant mixture with warm pita bread wedges. Garnish with lemon and lime slices, if desired. *Makes 4 servings*

Dietary Exchanges per Serving:
1 Starch/Bread, 1 Vegetable, ½ Fat

NUTRIENTS PER SERVING:
6 pita bread wedges; ½ cup eggplant spread

Calories	134
% calories from fat	20
Total Fat	3 g
Saturated Fat	<1 g
Cholesterol	0 mg
Sodium	347 mg
Carbohydrate	23 g
Dietary Fiber	3 g
Protein	4 g
Calcium	49 mg
Iron	2 mg
Vitamin A	87 RE
Vitamin C	18 mg

Tuna Salad Pita Pockets

1 (9-ounce) can tuna, drained
1 cup chopped cucumber
¼ cup part-skim ricotta cheese
2 tablespoons reduced fat
    mayonnaise
2 tablespoons red wine
    vinegar
2 green onions, chopped
1 tablespoon sweet pickle
    relish
2 cloves garlic, finely chopped
½ teaspoon salt
¼ teaspoon black pepper
1 cup alfalfa sprouts
2 pita breads, halved

Combine all ingredients except
sprouts. Fill bread with sprouts and
tuna.   *Makes 4 servings*

Dietary Exchanges per Serving:
1½ Starch/Bread, 2 Lean Meat

NUTRIENTS PER SERVING:

Calories	209
% calories from fat	18
Total Fat	4 g
Saturated Fat	1 g
Cholesterol	22 mg
Sodium	752 mg
Carbohydrate	22 g
Dietary Fiber	<1 g
Protein	22 g
Calcium	55 mg
Iron	1 mg
Vitamin A	44 RE
Vitamin C	4 mg

Cheesy Potato Skins

2 tablespoons grated
    Parmesan cheese
3 cloves garlic, finely chopped
2 teaspoons dried rosemary
½ teaspoon salt
¼ teaspoon black pepper
4 baked potatoes
2 egg whites, slightly beaten
½ cup (2 ounces) shredded
    part-skim mozzarella
    cheese

Preheat oven to 400°F. Combine
Parmesan cheese and seasonings.
Cut potatoes lengthwise in half.
Remove pulp, leaving ¼-inch-thick
shells. Cut lengthwise into wedges.
Place on baking sheet. Brush with
egg whites; sprinkle with cheese
mixture. Bake 20 minutes. Sprinkle
with mozzarella cheese; bake until
melted. Serve with salsa, if desired.
    Makes 8 servings

Dietary Exchanges per Serving:
1 Starch/Bread, ½ Lean Meat

NUTRIENTS PER SERVING:

Calories	90
% calories from fat	17
Total Fat	2 g
Saturated Fat	1 g
Cholesterol	5 mg
Sodium	215 mg
Carbohydrate	14 g
Dietary Fiber	2 g
Protein	5 g
Calcium	85 mg
Iron	2 mg
Vitamin A	17 RE
Vitamin C	5 mg

Tuna Salad Pita Pocket

Italian Meatball Subs

Nonstick cooking spray
½ cup chopped onion
3 teaspoons finely chopped
   garlic, divided
1 can (14½ ounces) Italian-
   style crushed tomatoes,
   undrained
2 bay leaves
2½ teaspoons dried basil
   leaves, divided
2 teaspoons dried oregano
   leaves, divided
¾ teaspoon ground black
   pepper, divided
¼ teaspoon crushed red
   pepper
½ pound lean ground beef
⅓ cup chopped green onions
⅓ cup dry bread crumbs
¼ cup chopped fresh parsley
1 egg white
½ teaspoon dried marjoram
   leaves
½ teaspoon ground mustard
4 French bread rolls, warmed,
   halved

1. Spray large nonstick saucepan with cooking spray. Heat over medium heat until hot. Add onion and 2 teaspoons garlic. Cook and stir 5 minutes or until onion is tender. Add tomatoes with liquid, bay leaves, 2 teaspoons basil, 1 teaspoon oregano, ½ teaspoon black pepper and red pepper; cover. Simmer 30 minutes, stirring occasionally. Remove and discard bay leaves.

2. Combine meat, green onions, bread crumbs, parsley, egg white, 2 tablespoons water, remaining 1 teaspoon garlic, ½ teaspoon basil, 1 teaspoon oregano, ¼ teaspoon black pepper, marjoram and mustard in medium bowl until well blended. Shape into 16 small meatballs.

3. Spray large nonstick skillet with cooking spray. Heat over medium heat until hot. Add meatballs. Cook 5 minutes or until meatballs are no longer pink in centers, turning occasionally.

4. Add meatballs to tomato sauce. Cook 5 minutes, stirring occasionally.

5. Place 4 meatballs in each roll. Spoon additional sauce over meatballs. Serve immediately.

Makes 4 servings

Dietary Exchanges per Serving:
2 Starch/Bread, 2 Lean Meat,
1 Vegetable

NUTRIENTS PER SERVING:

Calories	282
% calories from fat	30
Total Fat	9 g
Saturated Fat	3 g
Cholesterol	35 mg
Sodium	497 mg
Carbohydrate	32 g
Dietary Fiber	1 g
Protein	18 g
Calcium	134 mg
Iron	4 mg
Vitamin A	142 RE
Vitamin C	29 mg

Egg Rolls

Sweet and Sour Sauce
(recipe follows)
Nonstick cooking spray
3 green onions, finely
chopped
3 cloves garlic, finely chopped
½ teaspoon ground ginger
½ pound boneless skinless
chicken breasts, cooked,
finely chopped
2 cups bean sprouts, rinsed,
drained
½ cup shredded carrots
2 tablespoons reduced
sodium soy sauce
¼ teaspoon ground black
pepper
8 egg roll wrappers
2 teaspoons vegetable oil

1. Prepare Sweet and Sour Sauce.

2. Spray large nonstick skillet with cooking spray. Heat over medium-high heat until hot. Add onions, garlic and ginger. Cook and stir 1 minute. Add chicken, bean sprouts and carrots. Cook and stir 2 minutes. Stir in soy sauce and pepper. Cook and stir 1 minute. Remove skillet from heat. Let mixture stand 10 minutes or until cool enough to handle.

3. Brush edges of egg roll wrappers with water. Spoon filling evenly down centers of wrappers. Fold ends over fillings; roll up jelly-roll fashion.

4. Heat oil in another large nonstick skillet over medium heat until hot. Add rolls. Cook 3 to 5 minutes or until golden brown, turning occasionally. Serve hot with Sweet and Sour Sauce.

Makes 4 servings

Sweet and Sour Sauce

4 teaspoons cornstarch
1 cup water
½ cup sugar
½ cup white vinegar
¼ cup tomato paste

Combine all ingredients in small saucepan. Bring to a boil over high heat, stirring constantly. Boil 1 minute, stirring constantly. Cool.

Makes about 1½ cups (4 servings)

Dietary Exchanges per Serving:
1 Starch/Bread, 2 Lean Meat,
2 Vegetable

NUTRIENTS PER SERVING:
2 Egg Rolls

Calories	335
% calories from fat	13
Total Fat	5 g
Saturated Fat	<1 g
Cholesterol	48 mg
Sodium	465 mg
Carbohydrate	62 g
Dietary Fiber	5 g
Protein	25 g
Calcium	38 mg
Iron	3 mg
Vitamin A	455 RE
Vitamin C	17 mg

Miniature Fruit Muffins

1 cup whole wheat flour
¾ cup all-purpose flour
½ cup packed dark brown
  sugar
2 teaspoons baking powder
½ teaspoon baking soda
¼ teaspoon salt
1 cup buttermilk, divided
¾ cup frozen blueberries
1 small ripe banana, mashed
¼ teaspoon vanilla
⅓ cup unsweetened
  applesauce
2 tablespoons raisins
½ teaspoon ground cinnamon

1. Preheat oven to 400°F. Spray 36 miniature muffin cups with nonstick cooking spray; set aside.

2. Combine flours, sugar, baking powder, baking soda and salt in medium bowl. Place ⅓ cup dry ingredients in each of 2 small bowls.

3. To one portion flour mixture, add ⅓ cup buttermilk and blueberries. Stir just until blended; spoon into 12 prepared muffin cups. To second portion, add ⅓ cup buttermilk, banana and vanilla. Stir just until blended; spoon into 12 more prepared muffin cups. To final portion, add remaining ⅓ cup buttermilk, applesauce, raisins and cinnamon. Stir just until blended; spoon into remaining 12 prepared muffin cups.

4. Bake 18 minutes or until lightly browned and wooden pick inserted into centers comes out clean. Remove from pan. Cool 10 minutes on wire racks. Serve warm or cool completely.   *Makes 12 servings*

Dietary Exchanges per Serving:
1 Starch/Bread, 1 Fruit

NUTRIENTS PER SERVING:
3 miniature muffins

Calories	130
% calories from fat	4
Total Fat	1 g
Saturated Fat	<1 g
Cholesterol	1 mg
Sodium	178 mg
Carbohydrate	29 g
Dietary Fiber	2 g
Protein	3 g
Calcium	49 mg
Iron	1 mg
Vitamin A	4 RE
Vitamin C	2 mg

Super Soups & Salads

Crunch your way through crispy salads or spoon into splendid soups for a refreshing change of pace. Enjoy them on their own or as an appetizing prelude to a meal.

Apple Slaw with Poppy Seed Dressing

1 cup coarsely chopped unpeeled Jonathan apple
1 teaspoon lemon juice
2 tablespoons nonfat sour cream
4½ teaspoons skim milk
1 tablespoon frozen apple juice concentrate, thawed
1 teaspoon sugar
¾ teaspoon poppy seeds
½ cup sliced carrots
⅓ cup shredded green cabbage
⅓ cup shredded red cabbage
2 tablespoons finely chopped green bell pepper
Additional cabbage leaves (optional)

1. Combine apple and lemon juice in resealable plastic food storage bag. Seal bag; toss to coat.

2. Combine sour cream, milk, apple juice concentrate, sugar and poppy seeds in small bowl until well blended. Add apple mixture, carrots, cabbages and pepper; toss to coat. Serve on cabbage leaves and garnish with fresh greens and carrot slice, if desired.

Makes 2 servings

Dietary Exchanges per Serving:
1 Fruit, 1 Vegetable

NUTRIENTS PER SERVING:

Calories	94
% calories from fat	7
Total Fat	1 g
Saturated Fat	<1 g
Cholesterol	<1 mg
Sodium	34 mg
Carbohydrate	21 g
Dietary Fiber	2 g
Protein	3 g
Calcium	92 mg
Iron	1 mg
Vitamin A	375 RE
Vitamin C	44 mg

Apple Slaw with Poppy Seed Dressing

Vegetarian Chili

1 tablespoon vegetable oil
2 cloves garlic, finely chopped
1½ cups thinly sliced
    mushrooms
⅔ cup chopped red onion
⅔ cup chopped red bell pepper
2 teaspoons chili powder
¼ teaspoon ground cumin
⅛ teaspoon ground red pepper
⅛ teaspoon dried oregano
    leaves
1 can (28 ounces) peeled
    whole tomatoes
⅔ cup frozen baby lima beans
½ cup rinsed, drained canned
    Great Northern beans
3 tablespoons nonfat sour
    cream
3 tablespoons shredded
    reduced fat Cheddar
    cheese

1. Heat oil in large nonstick saucepan over medium-high heat until hot. Add garlic. Cook and stir 3 minutes. Add mushrooms, onion and bell pepper. Cook 5 minutes, stirring occasionally. Add chili powder, cumin, red pepper and oregano. Cook and stir 1 minute. Add tomatoes and beans. Reduce heat to medium-low. Simmer 15 minutes, stirring occasionally.

2. Top servings evenly with sour cream and cheese.

Makes 4 servings

Dietary Exchanges per Serving:
1 Starch/Bread, 3 Vegetable, 1 Fat

NUTRIENTS PER SERVING:

Calories	189
% calories from fat	24
Total Fat	5 g
Saturated Fat	1 g
Cholesterol	3 mg
Sodium	428 mg
Carbohydrate	29 g
Dietary Fiber	7 g
Protein	10 g
Calcium	154 mg
Iron	4 mg
Vitamin A	467 RE
Vitamin C	121 mg

Cook's Tip: To peel garlic easily, place a clove on a cutting board. Cover the clove with the flat side of a chef's knife blade, then firmly press down on the blade with your fist. This loosens the skin so that it comes right off.

Roasted Winter Vegetable Soup

1 small *or* ½ medium acorn
  squash, halved
2 medium tomatoes
1 medium onion, unpeeled
1 green bell pepper, halved
1 red bell pepper, halved
2 small red potatoes
3 cloves garlic, unpeeled
1½ cups tomato juice
4 teaspoons vegetable oil
1 tablespoon red wine vinegar
¼ teaspoon ground black
  pepper
¾ cup chopped fresh cilantro
4 tablespoons nonfat sour
  cream

1. Preheat oven to 400°F. Spray baking sheet with nonstick cooking spray.

2. Place acorn squash, tomatoes, onion, bell peppers, potatoes and garlic on prepared baking sheet. Bake 40 minutes, removing garlic and tomatoes after 10 minutes. Remove remaining vegetables from oven. Let stand 15 minutes or until cool enough to handle.

3. Peel vegetables and garlic; discard skins. Coarsely chop vegetables. Combine half of chopped vegetables, tomato juice, ½ cup water, oil and vinegar in food processor or blender; process until smooth.

4. Combine vegetable mixture, remaining chopped vegetables and black pepper in large saucepan. Bring to a simmer over medium-high heat. Simmer 5 minutes or until heated through, stirring constantly.

5. Top servings evenly with cilantro and sour cream.

Makes 4 servings

Dietary Exchanges per Serving:
1½ Starch/Bread, 2 Vegetable, 1 Fat

NUTRIENTS PER SERVING:

Calories	193
% calories from fat	22
Total Fat	5 g
Saturated Fat	<1 g
Cholesterol	0 mg
Sodium	345 mg
Carbohydrate	36 g
Dietary Fiber	5 g
Protein	5 g
Calcium	84 mg
Iron	2 mg
Vitamin A	330 RE
Vitamin C	92 mg

Mexicali Bean & Cheese Salad

1 teaspoon vegetable oil
1 clove garlic, finely chopped
¼ cup finely chopped red
  onion
1½ teaspoons chili powder
¼ teaspoon ground cumin
⅛ teaspoon crushed red
  pepper
1 boneless skinless chicken
  breast (about 6 ounces),
  cooked, shredded
1 cup frozen whole kernel
  corn, thawed
⅓ cup rinsed, drained canned
  pinto beans
⅓ cup rinsed, drained canned
  kidney beans
½ cup chopped seeded tomato
2 tablespoons drained canned
  diced mild green chilies
1 green onion, finely chopped
1 teaspoon lime juice
2 ounces reduced fat
  Monterey Jack cheese, cut
  into ⅓-inch cubes

1. Heat oil in medium nonstick skillet over medium heat until hot. Add garlic. Cook and stir 1 minute. Add red onion, chili powder, cumin and red pepper. Cook and stir 3 minutes. Add chicken, corn and beans. Cook 5 minutes or until heated through, stirring occasionally.

2. Spoon bean mixture into medium serving bowl. Add tomato, chilies, green onion and lime juice; toss to combine. Add cheese; toss to combine. Refrigerate 2 hours before serving. *Makes 2 servings*

Dietary Exchanges per Serving:
2½ Starch/Bread, 3 Lean Meat,
1 Vegetable

NUTRIENTS PER SERVING:

Calories	336
% calories from fat	25
Total Fat	10 g
Saturated Fat	4 g
Cholesterol	72 mg
Sodium	606 mg
Carbohydrate	36 g
Dietary Fiber	6 g
Protein	36 g
Calcium	310 mg
Iron	3 mg
Vitamin A	189 RE
Vitamin C	41 mg

Sunburst Chicken Salad

1 tablespoon fat free
    mayonnaise
1 tablespoon nonfat sour
    cream
2 teaspoons frozen orange
    juice concentrate, thawed
¼ teaspoon grated orange peel
1 boneless skinless chicken
    breast, cooked, chopped
1 large kiwi, thinly sliced
⅓ cup mandarin oranges
¼ cup finely chopped celery
4 lettuce leaves, washed
2 tablespoons coarsely
    chopped cashews

Combine mayonnaise, sour cream, concentrate and peel in small bowl. Add chicken, kiwi, oranges and celery; toss to coat. Cover; refrigerate 2 hours. Serve on lettuce leaves. Top with cashews.

Makes 2 servings

Dietary Exchanges per Serving:
2 Lean Meat, 1 Fruit, ½ Fat

NUTRIENTS PER SERVING:

Calories	195
% calories from fat	29
Total Fat	6 g
Saturated Fat	1 g
Cholesterol	39 mg
Sodium	431 mg
Carbohydrate	18 g
Dietary Fiber	2 g
Protein	18 g
Calcium	55 mg
Iron	1 mg

Salmon Pasta Salad

1 cup cooked medium shells
1 can (6 ounces) canned red
    salmon, rinsed, drained
½ cup finely chopped celery
2 tablespoons finely chopped
    red bell pepper
2 tablespoons chopped fresh
    parsley
2 tablespoons fat free
    mayonnaise
1 green onion, finely chopped
3 teaspoons lemon juice
2 teaspoons capers
⅛ teaspoon paprika

Combine all ingredients in medium bowl. Cover; refrigerate before serving. *Makes 2 servings*

Dietary Exchanges per Serving:
1½ Starch/Bread, 2 Lean Meat,
1 Vegetable, ½ Fat

NUTRIENTS PER SERVING:

Calories	262
% calories from fat	32
Total Fat	9 g
Saturated Fat	2 g
Cholesterol	21 mg
Sodium	627 mg
Carbohydrate	26 g
Dietary Fiber	2 g
Protein	18 g
Calcium	216 mg
Iron	2 mg
Vitamin A	153 RE
Vitamin C	44 mg

Sunburst Chicken Salad

Clam Chowder

1 can (5 ounces) whole baby
    clams, undrained
1 potato, peeled, coarsely
    chopped
¼ cup finely chopped onion
⅔ cup evaporated skim milk
    Pinch ground white pepper
    Pinch dried thyme leaves
1 tablespoon reduced calorie
    margarine

1. Drain clams; reserve juice. Add enough water to reserved juice to measure ⅔ cup. Combine clam juice mixture, potato and onion in large saucepan. Bring to a boil over high heat. Reduce heat to medium-low. Simmer 8 minutes or until potato is tender.

2. Add milk, pepper and thyme to saucepan. Increase heat to medium-high. Cook and stir 2 minutes. Add margarine. Cook 5 minutes or until soup thickens, stirring occasionally. Stir in clams.

Cook 5 minutes or until clams are firm, stirring occasionally. Garnish with red pepper strip, thyme and greens, if desired.

Makes 2 servings

Dietary Exchanges per Serving:
1 Starch/Bread, 1 Lean Meat, 1 Milk

NUTRIENTS PER SERVING:

Calories	204
% calories from fat	17
Total Fat	4 g
Saturated Fat	1 g
Cholesterol	47 mg
Sodium	205 mg
Carbohydrate	30 g
Dietary Fiber	1 g
Protein	14 g
Calcium	295 mg
Iron	3 mg
Vitamin A	164 RE
Vitamin C	9 mg

Health Note: A meal plan high in dietary calcium may actually prevent—not promote—the formation of kidney stones. Studies indicate that calcium, abundant in foods like milk, yogurt, cottage cheese and ricotta cheese, appears to bind oxalates that are linked to the formation of the stones.

Thai Pasta Salad with Peanut Sauce

¼ cup evaporated skim milk
4½ teaspoons creamy peanut butter
4½ teaspoons finely chopped red onion
1 teaspoon lemon juice
¾ teaspoon brown sugar
½ teaspoon reduced sodium soy sauce
⅛ teaspoon crushed red pepper
½ teaspoon finely chopped fresh ginger
1 cup hot cooked whole wheat spaghetti
2 teaspoons finely chopped green onion

1. Combine milk, peanut butter, red onion, lemon juice, sugar, soy sauce and red pepper in medium saucepan. Bring to a boil over high heat, stirring constantly. Boil 2 minutes, stirring constantly. Reduce heat to medium-low. Add ginger; blend well. Add spaghetti; toss to coat.

2. Top servings evenly with green onion. Serve immediately.
Makes 2 servings

Dietary Exchanges per Serving:
1½ Starch/Bread, ½ Milk, 1 Fat

NUTRIENTS PER SERVING:

Calories	187
% calories from fat	26
Total Fat	6 g
Saturated Fat	1 g
Cholesterol	38 mg
Sodium	85 mg
Carbohydrate	27 g
Dietary Fiber	3 g
Protein	9 g
Calcium	111 mg
Iron	1 mg
Vitamin A	45 RE
Vitamin C	3 mg

Cream of Chicken Soup

1 cup uncooked white rice
3 cans (10¾ ounces each)
 ⅓-less-salt chicken broth
1 skinless chicken breast
 (about 6 ounces)
1 rib celery, coarsely chopped
1 carrot, thinly sliced
¼ cup coarsely chopped onion
3 sprigs fresh parsley
1¼ cups evaporated skim milk
¼ teaspoon dried thyme leaves
⅛ teaspoon ground white
 pepper
⅛ teaspoon ground nutmeg
2 tablespoons finely chopped
 fresh parsley
1 green onion, finely chopped

1. Cook rice according to package directions, omitting salt.

2. Meanwhile, combine chicken broth and chicken in large saucepan. Bring to a boil over high heat. Reduce heat to medium-low. Simmer 10 minutes, skimming off any foam that rises to surface. Add celery, carrot, onion and parsley sprigs. Simmer 10 minutes or until chicken is no longer pink near bone and vegetables are tender, skimming off any foam that rises to surface.

3. Remove chicken breast from saucepan. Let stand 10 minutes or until cool enough to handle. Remove chicken from bone. Cut into 1-inch pieces.

4. Add rice, chicken pieces, milk, thyme, pepper and nutmeg to saucepan. Cook over medium-high heat 8 minutes or until soup thickens, stirring constantly.

5. Top servings evenly with finely chopped parsley and green onion.
Makes 4 servings

Dietary Exchanges per Serving:
2½ Starch/Bread, 1½ Lean Meat,
½ Milk, 1 Vegetable

NUTRIENTS PER SERVING:

Calories	326
% calories from fat	11
Total Fat	4 g
Saturated Fat	1 g
Cholesterol	28 mg
Sodium	173 mg
Carbohydrate	50 g
Dietary Fiber	1 g
Protein	21 g
Calcium	277 mg
Iron	3 mg
Vitamin A	633 RE
Vitamin C	11 mg

Zesty Taco Salad

2 tablespoons vegetable oil
1 clove garlic, finely chopped
¾ pound ground turkey
1¾ teaspoons chili powder
¼ teaspoon ground cumin
3 cups washed, torn lettuce
    leaves
1 can (14½ ounces) Mexican-
    style diced tomatoes,
    drained
1 cup rinsed, drained canned
    garbanzo beans (chick-
    peas) or pinto beans
⅔ cup chopped peeled
    cucumber
⅓ cup frozen whole kernel
    corn, thawed
¼ cup chopped red onion
1 to 2 jalapeño peppers,
    seeded, finely chopped*
    (optional)
1 tablespoon red wine vinegar
12 nonfat tortilla chips
    Fresh greens (optional)

* Jalapeño peppers can sting and irritate
the skin. Wear rubber gloves when
handling peppers and do not touch
eyes.

1. Combine oil and garlic in small
bowl; let stand 1 hour at room
temperature.

2. Combine turkey, chili powder and
cumin in large nonstick skillet. Cook
over medium heat 5 minutes or until
turkey is no longer pink, stirring to
crumble.

3. Combine turkey, lettuce,
tomatoes, beans, cucumber, corn,
onion and jalapeño in large bowl.
Remove garlic from oil; discard
garlic. Combine oil and vinegar in
small bowl. Drizzle over salad; toss
to coat. Serve on tortilla chips and
fresh greens, if desired. Serve with
additional tortilla chips and garnish
with cilantro, if desired.

Makes 4 servings

Dietary Exchanges per Serving:
1½ Starch/Bread, 2 Lean Meat,
1 Vegetable, 1 Fat

NUTRIENTS PER SERVING:

Calories	285
% calories from fat	33
Total Fat	11 g
Saturated Fat	1 g
Cholesterol	33 mg
Sodium	484 mg
Carbohydrate	28 g
Dietary Fiber	5 g
Protein	21 g
Calcium	77 mg
Iron	3 mg
Vitamin A	123 RE
Vitamin C	23 mg

Zesty Taco Salad

Delicious Dinners

Transform ho-hum meals into dynamite dinners with these mouthwatering entrées prepared with delicious Mexican, Oriental and Italian fixings.

Linguine with Pesto-Marinara Clam Sauce

1 teaspoon vegetable oil
¼ cup chopped shallots
3 cloves garlic, finely chopped
2 cans (6 ounces each) minced clams
1⅓ cups Marinara Sauce (page 55)
2 tablespoons prepared pesto sauce
¼ teaspoon crushed red pepper
8 ounces uncooked linguine
¼ cup chopped fresh parsley

1. Heat oil in large nonstick saucepan over medium heat until hot. Add shallots and garlic. Cook, covered, 2 minutes.

2. Drain clams; reserve ½ cup juice. Add clams, reserved juice, Marinara Sauce, pesto and red pepper to saucepan. Cook 10 minutes, stirring occasionally.

3. Prepare linguine according to package directions, omitting salt.

Drain. Spoon sauce evenly over each serving; top with parsley. Garnish with lemon slices and additional parsley, if desired.

Makes 4 servings

Dietary Exchanges per Serving:
2½ Starch/Bread, 3 Lean Meat, 2½ Vegetable

NUTRIENTS PER SERVING:

Calories	398
% calories from fat	13
Total Fat	6 g
Saturated Fat	1 g
Cholesterol	58 mg
Sodium	293 mg
Carbohydrate	54 g
Dietary Fiber	4 g
Protein	32 g
Calcium	146 mg
Iron	27 mg
Vitamin A	407 RE
Vitamin C	34 mg

Linguine with Pesto-Marinara Clam Sauce

Cashew Chicken

10 ounces boneless skinless
  chicken breasts, cut into
  1×½-inch pieces
1 tablespoon cornstarch
1 tablespoon dry white wine
1 tablespoon reduced sodium
  soy sauce
½ teaspoon garlic powder
1 teaspoon vegetable oil
6 green onions, cut into 1-inch
  pieces
2 cups sliced mushrooms
1 red or green bell pepper,
  thinly sliced
1 can (6 ounces) sliced water
  chestnuts, rinsed and
  drained
2 tablespoons hoisin sauce
  (optional)
2 cups hot cooked white rice
¼ cup roasted cashews

1. Place chicken in large resealable plastic food storage bag. Blend cornstarch, wine, soy sauce and garlic powder in small bowl. Pour over chicken pieces. Seal bag; turn to coat. Marinate in refrigerator 1 hour. Drain chicken; discard marinade.

2. Heat oil in wok or large nonstick skillet over medium-high heat until hot. Add onions; stir-fry 1 minute.

Add chicken; stir-fry 2 minutes or until browned. Add mushrooms, pepper and water chestnuts; stir-fry 3 minutes or until vegetables are crisp-tender and chicken is no longer pink in center. Stir in hoisin sauce; cook and stir 1 minute or until heated through.

3. Serve chicken and vegetables over rice. Top servings evenly with cashews. Serve immediately.
Makes 4 servings

Dietary Exchanges per Serving:
1½ Starch/Bread, 2 Lean Meat,
1½ Vegetable, ½ Fat

NUTRIENTS PER SERVING:

Calories	274
% calories from fat	23
Total Fat	7 g
Saturated Fat	1 g
Cholesterol	36 mg
Sodium	83 mg
Carbohydrate	34 g
Dietary Fiber	3 g
Protein	18 g
Calcium	28 mg
Iron	3 mg
Vitamin A	52 RE
Vitamin C	22 mg

Rio Grande Bean Enchiladas

3 teaspoons olive oil, divided
2 cups chopped onions,
  divided
1 can (14½ ounces) crushed
  tomatoes
1 can (6 ounces) tomato paste
2 tablespoons chili powder
1 tablespoon prepared green
  salsa
2 teaspoons ground cumin,
  divided
1 teaspoon sugar
⅛ teaspoon ground black
  pepper
2 cloves garlic, finely chopped
1 can (about 15 ounces) black
  beans, rinsed, drained,
  mashed
1 cup plain nonfat yogurt
8 (6-inch) corn tortillas

1. Heat 2 teaspoons oil in large saucepan over medium-high heat until hot. Add 1 cup onions. Cook and stir 5 minutes or until tender. Stir in tomatoes, tomato paste, chili powder, salsa, 1 teaspoon cumin, sugar and pepper. Reduce heat to medium-low. Simmer 30 minutes.

2. Heat remaining 1 teaspoon oil in large skillet over medium-high heat until hot. Add remaining 1 cup onions, 1 teaspoon cumin and garlic. Cook and stir 5 minutes or until onions are tender. Stir in beans. Cook 5 minutes or until heated through, stirring occasionally. Remove skillet from heat. Stir in yogurt.

3. Preheat oven to 375°F. Spoon bean mixture evenly down centers of tortillas. Roll up tortillas; place in medium baking dish. Top with sauce.

4. Bake 20 minutes. Serve with dollops of nonfat sour cream and cilantro, if desired. Garnish with cilantro and red pepper strips, if desired.   *Makes 4 servings*

Dietary Exchanges per Serving:
3 Starch/Bread, 4 Vegetable, 1½ Fat

NUTRIENTS PER SERVING:

Calories	365
% calories from fat	17
Total Fat	7 g
Saturated Fat	1 g
Cholesterol	1 mg
Sodium	1,050 mg
Carbohydrate	69 g
Dietary Fiber	11 g
Protein	19 g
Calcium	282 mg
Iron	4 mg
Vitamin A	315 RE
Vitamin C	44 mg

Fettuccine Alfredo

2 teaspoons margarine
3 cloves garlic, finely chopped
4½ teaspoons all-purpose flour
1½ cups skim milk
½ cup Parmesan cheese
3½ teaspoons Neufchâtel
     cheese
¼ teaspoon white pepper
4 ounces hot cooked
     fettuccine
¼ cup chopped fresh parsley

Melt margarine in medium saucepan. Add garlic. Cook and stir 1 minute. Stir in flour. Gradually stir in milk. Cook until sauce thickens, stirring constantly. Add cheeses and pepper; cook until melted. Serve on fettuccine; top with parsley.

Makes 4 servings

Dietary Exchanges per Serving:
2 Starch/Bread, 1 Lean Meat, 1 Fat

NUTRIENTS PER SERVING:

Calories	242
% calories from fat	33
Total Fat	9 g
Saturated Fat	4 g
Cholesterol	18 mg
Sodium	344 mg
Carbohydrate	27 g
Dietary Fiber	1 g
Protein	14 g
Calcium	307 mg
Iron	1 mg
Vitamin A	160 RE
Vitamin C	7 mg

Shrimp and Pineapple Kabobs

8 ounces medium shrimp,
     peeled and deveined
½ cup pineapple juice
¼ teaspoon garlic powder
12 chunks canned pineapple
1 green bell pepper, cut into
     1-inch pieces
¼ cup prepared chili sauce

1. Combine shrimp, juice and garlic powder in bowl; toss to coat. Marinate in refrigerator 30 minutes. Drain shrimp; discard marinade.

2. Alternately thread pineapple, pepper and shrimp onto 4 (10-inch) skewers. Brush with chili sauce. Grill, 4 inches from hot coals, 5 minutes or until shrimp are opaque, turning once and basting with chili sauce. *Makes 4 servings*

Dietary Exchanges per Serving:
1 Lean Meat, ½ Fruit, 1 Vegetable

NUTRIENTS PER SERVING:

Calories	100
% calories from fat	7
Total Fat	<1 g
Saturated Fat	<1 g
Cholesterol	87 mg
Sodium	302 mg
Carbohydrate	14 g
Dietary Fiber	1 g
Protein	10 g
Calcium	30 mg
Iron	2 mg
Vitamin A	94 RE
Vitamin C	61 mg

Beef & Vegetable Stir-Fry

½ cup ⅓-less-salt beef broth
3 tablespoons reduced sodium soy sauce
2 teaspoons cornstarch
1 teaspoon sugar
½ teaspoon ground ginger
½ teaspoon garlic powder
½ teaspoon Oriental sesame oil
¼ teaspoon salt
¼ teaspoon ground black pepper
1 teaspoon vegetable oil
½ pound beef flank steak, cut diagonally into 1-inch slices
2 green bell peppers, thinly sliced
1 tomato, cut into wedges
8 green onions, cut into 1-inch pieces
4 cups hot cooked white rice (optional)

1. Blend beef broth, soy sauce, cornstarch, sugar, ginger, garlic powder, sesame oil, salt and black pepper in medium bowl.

2. Heat vegetable oil in wok or nonstick skillet over medium-high heat until hot. Add beef; stir-fry 3 minutes or until beef is browned. Add bell peppers, tomato and onions; stir-fry 2 minutes or until vegetables are crisp-tender.

3. Stir beef broth mixture; add to wok. Cook and stir 3 minutes or until sauce boils and thickens.

4. Serve beef mixture over hot cooked white rice, if desired.

Makes 4 servings

Dietary Exchanges per Serving:
2½ Starch/Bread, 2 Lean Meat, 2 Vegetable

NUTRIENTS PER SERVING:

Calories	357
% calories from fat	15
Total Fat	6 g
Saturated Fat	2 g
Cholesterol	23 mg
Sodium	614 mg
Carbohydrate	54 g
Dietary Fiber	2 g
Protein	19 g
Calcium	35 mg
Iron	4 mg
Vitamin A	108 RE
Vitamin C	48 mg

Turkey Jambalaya

1 teaspoon vegetable oil
1 cup chopped onion
1 green bell pepper, chopped
½ cup chopped celery
3 cloves garlic, finely chopped
1¾ cups ⅓-less-salt chicken
    broth
1 cup chopped seeded tomato
¼ pound cooked ground
    turkey breast
¼ pound cooked turkey
    sausage
3 tablespoons tomato paste
1 bay leaf
1 teaspoon dried basil leaves
¼ teaspoon ground red pepper
1 cup uncooked white rice
¼ cup chopped fresh parsley

1. Heat oil in large nonstick skillet over medium-high heat until hot. Add onion, bell pepper, celery and garlic. Cook and stir 5 minutes or until vegetables are tender.

2. Add chicken broth, tomato, turkey, turkey sausage, tomato paste, bay leaf, basil and red pepper. Stir in rice. Bring to a boil over high heat, stirring occasionally. Reduce heat to medium-low. Simmer, covered, 20 minutes or until rice is tender.

3. Remove skillet from heat. Remove and discard bay leaf. Top servings evenly with parsley. Serve immediately. *Makes 4 servings*

Dietary Exchanges per Serving:
2½ Starch/Bread, 2 Lean Meat, 2½ Vegetable, ½ Fat

NUTRIENTS PER SERVING:

Calories	416
% calories from fat	18
Total Fat	9 g
Saturated Fat	2 g
Cholesterol	74 mg
Sodium	384 mg
Carbohydrate	51 g
Dietary Fiber	3 g
Protein	28 g
Calcium	84 mg
Iron	5 mg
Vitamin A	306 RE
Vitamin C	44 mg

Pork with Couscous & Root Vegetables

1 teaspoon vegetable oil
½ pound pork tenderloin, thinly sliced
2 sweet potatoes, peeled, chopped
2 medium turnips, peeled, chopped
1 carrot, sliced
3 cloves garlic, finely chopped
1 can (about 15 ounces) garbanzo beans (chick-peas), rinsed and drained
1 cup ⅓-less-salt vegetable broth
½ cup pitted prunes, cut into thirds
1 teaspoon ground cumin
½ teaspoon ground cinnamon
¼ teaspoon ground allspice
¼ teaspoon ground nutmeg
¼ teaspoon ground black pepper
1 cup uncooked quick-cooking couscous, cooked
2 tablespoons dried currants

1. Heat oil in large nonstick skillet over medium-high heat until hot. Add pork, sweet potatoes, turnips, carrot and garlic. Cook and stir 5 minutes. Stir in beans, vegetable broth, prunes, cumin, cinnamon, allspice, nutmeg and pepper. Cover; bring to a boil over high heat. Reduce heat to medium-low. Simmer 30 minutes.

2. Serve pork and vegetables on couscous. Top servings evenly with currants. Garnish with thyme, if desired. *Makes 4 servings*

Dietary Exchanges per Serving:
4 Starch/Bread, 2 Lean Meat, 1 Fruit, 2 Vegetable

NUTRIENTS PER SERVING:

Calories	508
% calories from fat	11
Total Fat	6 g
Saturated Fat	1 g
Cholesterol	30 mg
Sodium	500 mg
Carbohydrate	88 g
Dietary Fiber	17 g
Protein	26 g
Calcium	117 mg
Iron	5 mg
Vitamin A	1,793 RE
Vitamin C	28 mg

Health Note: Canola oil has the lowest percentage of saturated fat of any vegetable oil. Saturated fat interferes with the removal of excess fat and cholesterol from the body and should comprise only 10 percent of total calories (approximately 20 g for a 2,000 calorie diet).

Turkey Burgers

1 pound ground turkey breast
1 cup whole wheat bread
    crumbs
1 egg white
½ teaspoon dried sage leaves
½ teaspoon dried marjoram
    leaves
¼ teaspoon salt
¼ teaspoon ground black
    pepper
1 teaspoon vegetable oil
4 whole grain sandwich rolls,
    split in half
¼ cup Cowpoke Barbecue
    Sauce (page 60)*

*Or substitute prepared barbecue sauce.

1. Combine turkey, bread crumbs, egg white, sage, marjoram, salt and pepper in large bowl until well blended. Shape into 4 patties.

2. Heat oil in large nonstick skillet over medium-high heat until hot. Add patties. Cook 10 minutes or until patties are no longer pink in center, turning once.

3. Place one patty on bottom half of each roll. Spoon 1 tablespoon Cowpoke Barbecue Sauce over top of each burger. Place tops of rolls over burgers. Serve with lettuce and tomato and garnish with carrot slices, if desired.

Makes 4 burgers

Dietary Exchanges per Serving:
2 Starch/Bread, 3 Lean Meat

NUTRIENTS PER SERVING:

Calories	319
% calories from fat	17
Total Fat	6 g
Saturated Fat	1 g
Cholesterol	41 mg
Sodium	669 mg
Carbohydrate	40 g
Dietary Fiber	2 g
Protein	26 g
Calcium	116 mg
Iron	3 mg
Vitamin A	20 RE
Vitamin C	4 mg

Health Note: Too much fat—and too little—can seriously affect your health. The body needs a minimum of 15 to 25 grams a day, approximately 3 to 5 teaspoons, to carry out a variety of functions. Fat protects the body's vital organs, helps transport and store the vitamins A, D, E and K, and provides essential fatty acids that help maintain healthy skin.

Shrimp & Snow Peas with Fusilli

6 ounces uncooked fusilli
Nonstick cooking spray
2 cloves garlic, finely chopped
¼ teaspoon crushed red pepper
12 ounces medium shrimp, peeled and deveined
2 cups snow peas
1 can (8 ounces) sliced water chestnuts, drained
⅓ cup sliced green onions
3 tablespoons lime juice
2 tablespoons chopped fresh cilantro
2 tablespoons olive oil
1 tablespoon reduced sodium soy sauce
1½ teaspoons Mexican seasoning

1. Cook pasta according to package directions, omitting salt; drain. Set aside.

2. Spray large nonstick skillet with cooking spray; heat over medium heat until hot. Add garlic and red pepper; stir-fry 1 minute. Add shrimp; stir-fry 5 minutes or until shrimp are opaque. Remove shrimp from skillet.

3. Add snow peas and 2 tablespoons water to skillet; cook, covered, 1 minute. Uncover; cook and stir 2 minutes or until snow peas are crisp-tender. Remove snow peas from skillet.

4. Combine pasta, shrimp, snow peas, water chestnuts and onions in large bowl. Blend lime juice, cilantro, oil, soy sauce and Mexican seasoning in small bowl. Drizzle over pasta mixture; toss to coat. Garnish with radishes, if desired.

Makes 6 servings

Dietary Exchanges per Serving:
1½ Starch/Bread, 1 Lean Meat, 1 Vegetable, 1 Fat

NUTRIENTS PER SERVING:

Calories	228
% calories from fat	24
Total Fat	6 g
Saturated Fat	1 g
Cholesterol	87 mg
Sodium	202 mg
Carbohydrate	29 g
Dietary Fiber	3 g
Protein	15 g
Calcium	52 mg
Iron	4 mg
Vitamin A	92 RE
Vitamin C	36 mg

Grilled Tuna Niçoise with Citrus Marinade

Citrus Marinade (recipe follows)
1 tuna steak (about 1 pound)
2 cups green beans, trimmed, halved
4 cups romaine lettuce leaves, washed, torn into small pieces
8 small cooked red potatoes, quartered
1 cup chopped seeded tomato
4 cooked egg whites, chopped
¼ cup sliced red onion, halved
2 teaspoons chopped black olives

1. Prepare Citrus Marinade; combine with tuna in large resealable plastic food storage bag. Seal bag; turn to coat. Marinate in refrigerator 1 hour, turning occasionally.* Drain tuna; discard marinade.

2. To prevent sticking, spray grill with nonstick cooking spray. Prepare coals for grilling.

3. Place tuna on grill, 4 inches from hot coals. Grill 8 to 10 minutes or until tuna flakes easily when tested with fork, turning once. Or, place tuna on rack of broiler pan coated with nonstick cooking spray. Broil 4 inches from heat, 8 to 10 minutes or until tuna flakes easily when tested with fork. Slice tuna into ¼-inch-thick slices; set aside.

4. Place 2 cups water in large saucepan; bring to a boil over high heat. Add beans; cook 2 minutes. Drain; rinse with cold water and drain again.

5. Place lettuce on large serving platter. Arrange tuna, beans, potatoes, tomato, egg whites and onion on lettuce. Sprinkle servings with olives. Serve with low calorie salad dressing, if desired.

Makes 4 servings

*Marinate in refrigerator 1 hour for each inch of thickness.

Citrus Marinade

½ cup fresh lime juice
¼ cup vegetable oil
2 green onions, chopped
1 teaspoon dried tarragon leaves
¼ teaspoon garlic powder
¼ teaspoon ground black pepper

Blend all ingredients in small bowl.

Dietary Exchanges per Serving:
2 Starch/Bread, 3 Lean Meat, 2½ Vegetable

NUTRIENTS PER SERVING:

Calories	373
% calories from fat	16
Total Fat	7 g
Saturated Fat	1 g
Cholesterol	48 mg
Sodium	160 mg
Carbohydrate	45 g
Dietary Fiber	6 g
Protein	35 g
Calcium	92 mg
Iron	4 mg
Vitamin A	246 RE
Vitamin C	55 mg

Spaghetti with Marinara Sauce

MARINARA SAUCE

- 1 teaspoon olive oil
- ¾ cup chopped onion
- 3 cloves garlic, finely chopped
- 1 can (16 ounces) no-salt-added tomato sauce
- 1 can (6 ounces) tomato paste
- 2 bay leaves
- 1 teaspoon dried oregano
- 1 teaspoon dried basil
- ½ teaspoon dried marjoram
- ½ teaspoon honey
- ¼ teaspoon black pepper

  8 ounces uncooked spaghetti, cooked, drained, kept hot

1. Heat oil in large saucepan. Add onion and garlic. Cook and stir 5 minutes or until onion is tender. Add 2 cups water, tomato sauce, tomato paste, bay leaves, oregano, basil, marjoram, honey and pepper. Bring to a boil, stirring occasionally. Reduce heat; simmer 1 hour, stirring occasionally.

2. Remove and discard bay leaves. Measure 2 cups sauce; reserve remaining sauce for another use. Serve sauce on pasta.

Makes 4 servings

Dietary Exchanges per Serving:
3 Starch/Bread, 2½ Vegetable

NUTRIENTS PER SERVING:

Calories	289
% calories from fat	<1
Total Fat	2 g
Saturated Fat	<1 g
Cholesterol	0 mg
Sodium	213 mg
Carbohydrate	68 g
Dietary Fiber	3 g
Protein	10 g
Calcium	41 mg
Iron	4 mg
Vitamin A	126 RE
Vitamin C	20 mg

Spinach-Stuffed Shells

1 package (10 ounces) chopped frozen spinach, thawed and drained
1½ cups nonfat ricotta cheese
½ cup grated Parmesan cheese
½ cup cholesterol free egg substitute
3 cloves garlic, finely chopped
1 teaspoon dried oregano leaves
½ teaspoon salt
½ teaspoon dried basil leaves
½ teaspoon dried marjoram leaves
¼ teaspoon ground black pepper
24 cooked large pasta shells
2 cans (14½ ounces each) crushed tomatoes
1 cup (4 ounces) shredded reduced fat mozzarella cheese

1. Preheat oven to 350°F. Spray 13×9-inch baking pan with nonstick cooking spray.

2. Combine spinach, ricotta and Parmesan cheeses, egg substitute and seasonings in large bowl. Spoon into shells. Place shells in prepared pan. Top with tomatoes with liquid and mozzarella cheese. Bake 20 minutes or until cheese melts.   *Makes 4 servings*

Dietary Exchanges per Serving:
3 Starch/Bread, 3 Lean Meat, 2 Vegetable

NUTRIENTS PER SERVING:

Calories	456
% calories from fat	20
Total Fat	11 g
Saturated Fat	6 g
Cholesterol	35 mg
Sodium	803 mg
Carbohydrate	57 g
Dietary Fiber	6 g
Protein	38 g
Calcium	684 mg
Iron	5 mg
Vitamin A	1,081 RE
Vitamin C	41 mg

Health Note: Recent studies have shown that garlic may play a role in the prevention of heart disease. Results indicate that a clove a day may lower levels of bad cholesterol (LDL), may help prevent the formation of blood clots that lead to heart attacks and strokes, and may aid in lowering high blood pressure levels.

Lemon-Crusted Country Pie

½ cup plus 2 tablespoons
    all-purpose flour, divided
⅓ cup whole wheat flour
1 teaspoon grated lemon peel
2 tablespoons vegetable oil
3 to 4 tablespoons ice water
    Nonstick cooking spray
1 boneless skinless chicken
    breast, chopped
1 cup chopped onion
1 cup chopped celery
1 cup sliced mushrooms
½ cup shredded carrot
1 tablespoon margarine
½ cup ⅓-less-salt chicken broth
½ cup skim milk
½ teaspoon salt
½ teaspoon dried rosemary
¼ teaspoon ground black
    pepper
1 cup frozen whole kernel corn
1 cup frozen green peas
⅓ cup whole wheat bread
    crumbs

1. Combine ½ cup all-purpose flour, whole wheat flour and lemon peel in medium bowl. Add oil; blend well. Add water, 1 tablespoon at a time, until soft dough forms. Flatten dough into disc; cover with plastic wrap. Refrigerate 30 minutes.

2. Place dough on lightly floured surface. Roll out dough into 10-inch circle, ⅛ inch thick. Ease dough into 9-inch pie plate. (If excess dough remains, reroll and cut out decorative shapes.)

3. Spray large skillet with cooking spray. Add chicken. Cook and stir 3 minutes. Add vegetables. Cook and stir 5 minutes or until chicken is no longer pink. Set aside.

4. Preheat oven to 375°F. Melt margarine in medium saucepan over medium heat. Add remaining 2 tablespoons flour. Cook and stir 3 minutes. Gradually stir in chicken broth, milk, salt, rosemary and pepper. Cook 6 minutes or until sauce thickens, stirring constantly. Stir in chicken mixture, corn, peas and bread crumbs. Remove saucepan from heat; let stand 15 minutes.

5. Spoon vegetable mixture into prepared crust. (Arrange cutouts over top of pie, if desired.) Brush with additional milk.

6. Bake 50 minutes or until filling is set. (If crust browns too much before filling sets, cover with strips of aluminum foil.)

Makes 4 servings

Dietary Exchanges per Serving:
2½ Starch/Bread, 1 Lean Meat,
2 Vegetable, 2 Fat

NUTRIENTS PER SERVING:

Calories	372
% calories from fat	29
Total Fat	12 g
Saturated Fat	2 g
Cholesterol	28 mg
Sodium	449 mg
Carbohydrate	47 g
Dietary Fiber	6 g
Protein	19 g
Calcium	97 mg
Iron	3 mg
Vitamin A	540 RE
Vitamin C	13 mg

Lemon-Crusted Country Pie

Chicken Fajitas with Cowpoke Barbecue Sauce

1 cup Cowpoke Barbecue
　Sauce (recipe follows),
　divided
Nonstick cooking spray
10 ounces boneless skinless
　chicken breasts, cut
　lengthwise into 1×½-inch
　pieces
2 green or red bell peppers,
　thinly sliced
1 cup sliced onion
2 cups tomato wedges
4 (6-inch) warm flour tortillas

1. Prepare Cowpoke Barbecue
Sauce.

2. Spray large nonstick skillet with
cooking spray. Heat over medium-
high heat until hot. Brush chicken
with ¼ cup barbecue sauce. Add to
skillet. Cook and stir 3 minutes or
until chicken is browned. Add
peppers and onion. Cook and stir
3 minutes or until vegetables are
crisp-tender and chicken is no
longer pink. Add tomatoes. Cook
2 minutes or until heated through,
stirring occasionally.

3. Serve with warm flour tortillas
and remaining ¾ cup Cowpoke
Barbecue Sauce. Garnish with
cilantro, if desired.

Makes 4 servings

Cowpoke Barbecue Sauce

1 teaspoon vegetable oil
¾ cup chopped green onions
3 cloves garlic, finely chopped
1 can (14½ ounces) crushed
　tomatoes
½ cup ketchup
¼ cup water
¼ cup orange juice
2 tablespoons cider vinegar
2 teaspoons chili sauce
Dash Worcestershire sauce

Heat oil in large nonstick saucepan
over medium heat until hot. Add
onions and garlic. Cook and stir 5
minutes or until onions are tender.
Stir in remaining ingredients.
Reduce heat to medium-low. Cook
15 minutes, stirring occasionally.

Makes 2 cups

Dietary Exchanges per Serving:
1½ Starch/Bread, 2 Lean Meat,
2½ Vegetable

NUTRIENTS PER SERVING:

Calories	310
% calories from fat	18
Total Fat	6 g
Saturated Fat	1 g
Cholesterol	36 mg
Sodium	736 mg
Carbohydrate	47 g
Dietary Fiber	4 g
Protein	20 g
Calcium	104 mg
Iron	3 mg
Vitamin A	259 RE
Vitamin C	90 mg

*Chicken Fajitas with Cowpoke
Barbecue Sauce*

Paella

Nonstick cooking spray
10 ounces boneless skinless
    chicken breasts
1 teaspoon vegetable oil
½ cup uncooked white rice
4 cloves garlic, finely chopped
½ cup sliced onion
½ cup sliced green bell pepper
1 cup ⅓-less salt chicken
    broth
½ teaspoon ground turmeric
¼ teaspoon salt
¼ teaspoon paprika
¼ teaspoon ground black
    pepper
½ cup frozen green peas
½ cup drained canned diced
    tomatoes
8 ounces medium shrimp,
    peeled

1. Preheat oven to 350°F. Spray large skillet with cooking spray; heat over medium-high heat until hot. Add chicken. Cook 10 minutes or until chicken is no longer pink in center, turning once. Remove chicken from skillet. Cool 10 minutes or until cool enough to handle. Cut into 1-inch pieces.

2. Heat oil in large ovenproof skillet or paella pan over medium heat until hot. Add rice and garlic. Cook 5 minutes or until rice is browned, stirring occasionally. Add onion and bell pepper. Stir in chicken broth, turmeric, salt, paprika and black pepper. Stir in peas and tomatoes. Place chicken and shrimp on top of rice mixture.

3. Bake 20 minutes or until heated through. Let stand 5 minutes before serving. *Makes 4 servings*

Dietary Exchanges per Serving:
1½ Starch/Bread, 3 Lean Meat,
1 Vegetable

NUTRIENTS PER SERVING:

Calories	258
% calories from fat	14
Total Fat	4 g
Saturated Fat	1 g
Cholesterol	123 mg
Sodium	371 mg
Carbohydrate	28 g
Dietary Fiber	2 g
Protein	27 g
Calcium	51 mg
Iron	4 mg
Vitamin A	95 RE
Vitamin C	36 mg

Tamale Pie

BISCUIT TOPPING
- ½ cup white or yellow cornmeal
- ½ cup buttermilk
- ⅓ cup all-purpose flour
- 1 egg white, slightly beaten
- 1 tablespoon sugar
- ½ jalapeño pepper, seeded, chopped*
- 1 teaspoon baking powder

FILLING
- Nonstick cooking spray
- 1 green bell pepper, chopped
- ¾ cup chopped green onions
- 2 cloves garlic, finely chopped
- 1½ cups canned crushed tomatoes
- 1 can (about 15 ounces) pinto beans, rinsed and drained
- ¼ pound cooked ground turkey breast
- 2 teaspoons chili powder
- 1 teaspoon ground cumin
- ¼ teaspoon ground black pepper

*Jalapeño peppers can sting and irritate the skin. Wear rubber gloves when handling peppers and do not touch eyes.

1. Preheat oven to 425°F. Spray 9-inch pie plate with nonstick cooking spray; set aside.

2. For topping, combine all topping ingredients in large bowl until well blended; set aside.

3. For filling, spray large nonstick skillet with cooking spray. Heat over medium heat until hot. Add bell pepper, onions and garlic. Cook and stir 5 minutes or until vegetables are tender. Add tomatoes, beans, turkey, chili powder, cumin and black pepper. Cook and stir 5 minutes or until heated through.

4. Spoon vegetable mixture into prepared pie plate. Drop heaping tablespoonfuls topping around outer edge of filling; flatten with back of spoon to form biscuits.

5. Bake 25 minutes or until biscuits are golden brown. Let stand 5 minutes before serving.

Makes 4 servings

Dietary Exchanges per Serving:
2½ Starch/Bread, 1 Lean Meat, 1 Vegetable

NUTRIENTS PER SERVING:

Calories	274
% calories from fat	13
Total Fat	4 g
Saturated Fat	1 g
Cholesterol	12 mg
Sodium	750 mg
Carbohydrate	47 g
Dietary Fiber	4 g
Protein	14 g
Calcium	140 mg
Iron	5 mg
Vitamin A	199 RE
Vitamin C	45 mg

Stir-Fried Pork Lo Mein

Nonstick cooking spray
6 green onions, cut into 1-inch pieces
½ teaspoon garlic powder
½ teaspoon ground ginger
6 ounces pork loin roast, thinly sliced
3 cups shredded green cabbage
½ cup shredded carrots
½ cup trimmed snow peas
½ cup ⅓-less-salt chicken broth
2 teaspoons cornstarch
2 tablespoons hoisin sauce (optional)
1 tablespoon reduced sodium soy sauce
8 ounces hot cooked linguine

1. Spray wok with cooking spray. Heat over medium heat until hot. Add onions, garlic powder and ginger; stir-fry 30 seconds. Add pork; stir-fry 2 minutes or until pork is no longer pink. Add vegetables; stir-fry 3 minutes or until vegetables are crisp-tender.

2. Blend chicken broth, cornstarch, hoisin sauce and soy sauce in small bowl. Add to wok. Cook and stir until mixture boils and thickens. Serve vegetables and sauce over pasta.   *Makes 4 servings*

Dietary Exchanges per Serving:
3 Starch/Bread, 1 Lean Meat, 1½ Vegetable

NUTRIENTS PER SERVING:

Calories	310
% calories from fat	13
Total Fat	4 g
Saturated Fat	1 g
Cholesterol	25 mg
Sodium	228 mg
Carbohydrate	48 g
Dietary Fiber	4 g
Protein	20 g
Calcium	66 mg
Iron	3 mg
Vitamin A	445 RE
Vitamin C	48 mg

Health Note: An estimated 50 percent of older adults rely on nonbulk forming laxatives for regularity. Frequent use of these laxatives lowers the level of the blood protein albumin. Research suggests that lower than normal albumin levels may increase your risk of heart disease and cancer. Instead, try a more natural approach to regularity—increase your intake of fluids and fiber-rich foods such as whole grains, fruits and vegetables, and increase your level of physical activity.

Versatile Vegetables & Sides

Pick-of-the-crop vegetables star in this magnificent chapter. Discover your low fat, high fiber favorites tucked into scrumptious sides or packed into memorable main dishes.

Green Pea & Rice Almondine

2 teaspoons reduced calorie margarine
1 cup frozen baby green peas
¼ teaspoon ground cardamom
¼ teaspoon ground cinnamon
Pinch ground cloves
Pinch ground white pepper
¾ cup cooked white rice
2 teaspoons slivered almonds

Melt margarine in medium nonstick skillet over medium heat. Add peas, cardamom, cinnamon, cloves and pepper. Cook and stir 10 minutes or until peas are tender. Add rice. Cook until heated through, stirring occasionally. Sprinkle almonds evenly over servings.

Makes 4 servings

Dietary Exchanges per Serving:
1 Starch/Bread, ½ Fat

NUTRIENTS PER SERVING:

Calories	100
% calories from fat	16
Total Fat	2 g
Saturated Fat	<1 g
Cholesterol	0 mg
Sodium	57 mg
Carbohydrate	18 g
Dietary Fiber	2 g
Protein	3 g
Calcium	19 mg
Iron	1 mg
Vitamin A	48 RE
Vitamin C	4 mg

Broccoli with Creamy Lemon Sauce

2 tablespoons fat free
   mayonnaise
4½ teaspoons low fat sour
   cream
1 tablespoon skim milk
1 to 1½ teaspoons lemon juice
⅛ teaspoon ground turmeric
1¼ cups hot cooked broccoli
   flowerets

Combine all ingredients except broccoli in top of double boiler. Cook over simmering water 5 minutes or until heated through, stirring constantly. Serve over hot cooked broccoli.

Makes 2 servings

Dietary Exchanges per Serving:
2 Vegetable

NUTRIENTS PER SERVING:

Calories	44
% calories from fat	18
Total Fat	1 g
Saturated Fat	<1 g
Cholesterol	4 mg
Sodium	216 mg
Carbohydrate	7 g
Dietary Fiber	2 g
Protein	2 g
Calcium	50 mg
Iron	1 mg
Vitamin A	132 RE
Vitamin C	53 mg

Zucchini Cakes

3 teaspoons reduced calorie
   margarine, divided
2 tablespoons finely chopped
   red onion
1 zucchini
½ baking potato, peeled
¼ cup cholesterol free egg
   substitute
4½ teaspoons bread crumbs
1 teaspoon chopped dill
   Pinch ground white pepper

1. Melt 1½ teaspoons margarine in large skillet. Add onion; cook and stir 5 minutes or until tender.

2. Shred zucchini and potato with grater. Drain. Combine onion, zucchini, potato, egg substitute, bread crumbs, dill and pepper in medium bowl.

3. Melt remaining 1½ teaspoons margarine in large skillet. Drop 4 heaping ¼-cupfuls mixture into skillet; flatten. Cook 10 minutes or until golden brown, turning once.

Makes 2 servings

Dietary Exchanges per Serving:
1 Starch/Bread, ½ Vegetable, ½ Fat

NUTRIENTS PER SERVING:

Calories	111
% calories from fat	24
Total Fat	3 g
Saturated Fat	1 g
Cholesterol	0 mg
Sodium	123 mg
Carbohydrate	17 g
Dietary Fiber	1 g
Protein	5 g
Calcium	26 mg
Iron	1 mg
Vitamin A	239 RE
Vitamin C	14 mg

Potatoes au Gratin

1 pound baking potatoes
4 teaspoons reduced calorie
   margarine
4 teaspoons all-purpose flour
1¼ cups skim milk
¼ teaspoon ground nutmeg
¼ teaspoon paprika
   Pinch ground white pepper
½ cup thinly sliced red onion,
   divided
⅓ cup whole wheat bread
   crumbs
1 tablespoon finely chopped
   red onion
1 tablespoon grated
   Parmesan cheese

1. Spray 4- or 6-cup casserole with nonstick cooking spray; set aside.

2. Place potatoes in large saucepan; add water to cover. Bring to a boil over high heat. Boil 12 minutes or until potatoes are tender. Drain; let potatoes stand 10 minutes or until cool enough to handle.

3. Melt margarine in small saucepan over medium heat. Add flour. Cook and stir 3 minutes or until small clumps form. Gradually whisk in milk. Cook 8 minutes or until sauce thickens, stirring constantly. Remove saucepan from heat. Stir in nutmeg, paprika and pepper.

4. Preheat oven to 350°F. Cut potatoes into thin slices. Arrange half of potato slices in prepared casserole. Sprinkle with half of onion slices. Repeat layers. Spoon sauce over potato mixture. Combine bread crumbs, finely chopped red onion and cheese in small bowl. Sprinkle mixture evenly over sauce.

5. Bake 20 minutes. Let stand 5 minutes before serving. Garnish as desired.   *Makes 4 servings*

Dietary Exchanges per Serving:
2 Starch/Bread, ½ Vegetable, ½ Fat

NUTRIENTS PER SERVING:

Calories	178
% calories from fat	14
Total Fat	3 g
Saturated Fat	1 g
Cholesterol	2 mg
Sodium	144 mg
Carbohydrate	33 g
Dietary Fiber	2 g
Protein	6 g
Calcium	135 mg
Iron	1 mg
Vitamin A	103 RE
Vitamin C	10 mg

Spaghetti Squash Primavera

2 teaspoons vegetable oil
½ teaspoon finely chopped garlic
¼ cup finely chopped red onion
¼ cup thinly sliced carrot
¼ cup thinly sliced red bell pepper
¼ cup thinly sliced green bell pepper
1 can (14½ ounces) Italian-style stewed tomatoes
½ cup thinly sliced yellow squash
½ cup thinly sliced zucchini
½ cup frozen whole kernel corn, thawed
½ teaspoon dried oregano leaves
⅛ teaspoon dried thyme leaves
1 spaghetti squash (about 2 pounds)
4 teaspoons grated Parmesan cheese (optional)
2 tablespoons finely chopped fresh parsley

1. Heat oil in large skillet over medium-high heat until hot. Add garlic. Cook and stir 3 minutes. Add onion, carrot and peppers. Cook and stir 3 minutes. Add tomatoes, squash, zucchini, corn, oregano and thyme. Cook 5 minutes or until heated through, stirring occasionally.

2. Cut squash lengthwise in half. Remove seeds. Cover with plastic wrap. Microwave at HIGH 9 minutes or until squash separates easily into strands when tested with fork.

3. Cut each squash half lengthwise in half; separate strands with fork. Spoon vegetables evenly over squash. Top servings evenly with cheese, if desired and parsley before serving.

Makes 4 servings

Dietary Exchanges per Serving:
1 Starch/Bread, 1 Vegetable, ½ Fat

NUTRIENTS PER SERVING:

Calories	101
% calories from fat	25
Total Fat	3 g
Saturated Fat	<1 g
Cholesterol	0 mg
Sodium	11 mg
Carbohydrate	18 g
Dietary Fiber	5 g
Protein	3 g
Calcium	70 mg
Iron	1 mg
Vitamin A	309 RE
Vitamin C	48 mg

Broccoli & Cauliflower Stir-Fry

2 dry-pack sun-dried
   tomatoes
4 teaspoons reduced sodium
   soy sauce
1 tablespoon rice wine vinegar
1 teaspoon brown sugar
1 teaspoon Oriental sesame
   oil
⅛ teaspoon crushed red
   pepper
2¼ teaspoons vegetable oil
2 cups cauliflowerets
2 cups broccoli flowerets
1 clove garlic, finely chopped
⅓ cup thinly sliced red or
   green bell pepper

1. Place tomatoes in small bowl; cover with boiling water. Let stand 5 minutes. Drain; coarsely chop. Meanwhile, blend soy sauce, vinegar, sugar, sesame oil and red pepper in small bowl.

2. Heat vegetable oil in wok or large nonstick skillet over medium-high heat until hot. Add cauliflower, broccoli and garlic; stir-fry 4 minutes. Add tomatoes and bell pepper; stir-fry 1 minute or until vegetables are crisp-tender. Add soy sauce mixture; cook and stir until heated through. Serve immediately.   *Makes 2 servings*

Dietary Exchanges per Serving:
6 Vegetable, 1½ Fat

NUTRIENTS PER SERVING:

Calories	214
% calories from fat	30
Total Fat	8 g
Saturated Fat	1 g
Cholesterol	0 mg
Sodium	443 mg
Carbohydrate	32 g
Dietary Fiber	5 g
Protein	9 g
Calcium	115 mg
Iron	3 mg
Vitamin A	1,493 RE
Vitamin C	249 mg

Health Tip: Learning to identify low-fat food items on a menu is an easy way to plan a healthy meal when dining out. Phrases such as broiled, grilled, roasted, stir-fried, and steamed are often used to describe foods that are prepared with less fat. Limit entrées that are buttered, basted, fried, or creamed—these foods are usually prepared with significant amounts of fat.

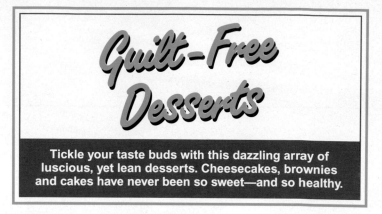

Tickle your taste buds with this dazzling array of luscious, yet lean desserts. Cheesecakes, brownies and cakes have never been so sweet—and so healthy.

Brownie Cake Delight

- 1 package reduced fat fudge brownie mix
- ⅓ cup strawberry all fruit spread
- 2 cups thawed reduced fat nondairy whipped topping
- ¼ teaspoon almond extract
- 2 cups strawberries, stems removed, halved
- ¼ cup chocolate sauce

1. Prepare brownies according to package directions, substituting 11×7-inch baking pan. Cool completely in pan.

2. Whisk fruit spread in small bowl until smooth.

3. Combine whipped topping and almond extract in medium bowl.

4. Cut brownie crosswise in half. Place half of brownie, flat-side down, on serving dish. Spread with fruit spread and 1 cup whipped topping. Place second half of brownie, flat-side down, over bottom layer. Spread with remaining whipped topping. Arrange strawberries on whipped topping. Drizzle chocolate sauce onto cake before serving. Garnish with fresh mint, if desired.

Makes 16 servings

Dietary Exchanges per Serving:
2 Starch/Bread, ½ Fruit, ½ Fat

NUTRIENTS PER SERVING:

Calories	193
% calories from fat	14
Total Fat	3 g
Saturated Fat	<1 g
Cholesterol	<1 mg
Sodium	140 mg
Carbohydrate	41 g
Dietary Fiber	<1 g
Protein	2 g
Calcium	11 mg
Iron	1 mg
Vitamin A	11 RE
Vitamin C	11 mg

Cheese-Filled Poached Pears

1½ quarts cranberry-raspberry juice cocktail
2 ripe Bartlett pears with stems, peeled
2 tablespoons Neufchâtel cheese
2 teaspoons crumbled Gorgonzola cheese
1 tablespoon chopped walnuts

1. Bring juice to a boil in medium saucepan over high heat. Add pears; reduce heat to medium-low. Simmer 15 minutes or until pears are tender, turning occasionally. Remove pears from saucepan; discard liquid. Let stand 10 minutes or until cool enough to handle.

2. Combine cheeses in small bowl until well blended. Cut thin slice off bottom of each pear so that pears stand evenly. Cut pears lengthwise in half, leaving stems intact. Scoop out seeds and membranes to form small hole in each pear half. Fill holes with cheese mixture; press halves together. Place nuts in large bowl; roll pears in nuts to coat. Cover; refrigerate until ready to serve.   *Makes 2 servings*

Dietary Exchanges per Serving:
½ Lean Meat, 3 Fruit, 1 Fat

NUTRIENTS PER SERVING:

Calories	240
% calories from fat	24
Total Fat	7 g
Saturated Fat	3 g
Cholesterol	13 mg
Sodium	98 mg
Carbohydrate	45 g
Dietary Fiber	4 g
Protein	4 g
Calcium	53 mg
Iron	1 mg
Vitamin A	58 RE
Vitamin C	41 mg

Health Tip: Start your search for healthy fare by scouting the front panel of food packages for nutritional claims. Manufacturers that adhere to strict definitions set by the government can advertise information about their products with phrases like "Low Fat," "Fat Free," "Good Source of Calcium" and "Sodium Free," which makes it easier for consumers to plan healthful meals.

Cheese-Filled Poached Pear

Chocolate Angel Fruit Torte

1 package chocolate angel
   food cake mix
2 bananas, thinly sliced
1½ teaspoons lemon juice
1 can (12 ounces) evaporated
   skim milk, divided
⅓ cup sugar
¼ cup cornstarch
⅓ cup cholesterol free egg
   substitute
3 tablespoons nonfat sour
   cream
3 teaspoons vanilla
3 large kiwis, peeled, thinly
   sliced
1 can (11 ounces) mandarin
   orange segments, rinsed,
   drained

1. Prepare cake according to package directions; cool completely. Cut horizontally in half to form 2 layers; set aside.

2. Place banana slices in medium bowl. Add lemon juice; toss to coat. Set aside.

3. Combine ¼ cup milk, sugar and cornstarch in small saucepan; whisk until smooth. Whisk in remaining milk. Bring to a boil over high heat, stirring constantly. Boil 1 minute or until mixture thickens, stirring constantly. Reduce heat to medium-low.

4. Blend ⅓ cup hot milk mixture and egg substitute in small bowl. Add to saucepan. Cook 2 minutes, stirring constantly. Remove saucepan from heat. Let stand 10 minutes, stirring frequently. Add sour cream and vanilla; blend well.

5. Place bottom half of cake on serving plate. Spread with half of milk mixture. Arrange half of banana slices, kiwi slices and mandarin orange segments on milk mixture. Place remaining half of cake, cut-side down, over fruit. Top with remaining milk mixture and fruit. *Makes 12 servings*

Dietary Exchanges per Serving:
2½ Starch/Bread, 1 Fruit

NUTRIENTS PER SERVING:

Calories	233
% calories from fat	1
Total Fat	<1 g
Saturated Fat	<1 g
Cholesterol	1 mg
Sodium	306 mg
Carbohydrate	52 g
Dietary Fiber	1 g
Protein	7 g
Calcium	150 mg
Iron	1 mg
Vitamin A	113 RE
Vitamin C	30 mg

Sour Cream Apple Tart

5 tablespoons reduced calorie margarine, divided
¾ cup graham cracker crumbs
1¼ teaspoons ground cinnamon, divided
1⅓ cups low fat sour cream
¾ cup sugar, divided
½ cup all-purpose flour, divided
½ cup cholesterol free egg substitute
1 teaspoon vanilla
5 cups coarsely chopped peeled Jonathan apples or other firm red-skinned apples

1. Preheat oven to 350°F.

2. Melt 3 tablespoons margarine in small saucepan over medium heat. Stir in graham cracker crumbs and ¼ teaspoon cinnamon until well blended. Press crumb mixture firmly onto bottom of 9-inch springform pan. Bake 10 minutes. Remove from oven; cool.

3. Combine sour cream, ½ cup sugar and 2 tablespoons plus 1½ teaspoons flour in large bowl with electric mixer. Beat at medium speed until well blended. Beat in egg substitute and vanilla until well blended. Stir in chopped apples with spoon. Spoon apple mixture into prepared crust.

4. Bake 35 minutes or until center is just set.

5. Preheat broiler. Combine remaining 1 teaspoon cinnamon, ¼ cup sugar and 5 tablespoons plus 1½ teaspoons flour in small bowl. Cut in remaining 2 tablespoons margarine with pastry blender until mixture resembles coarse crumbs. Sprinkle mixture evenly over top of fruit.

6. Broil 3 to 4 minutes or until topping is golden brown. Remove from oven. Let stand 15 minutes before serving.

Makes 12 servings

Dietary Exchanges per Serving:
1½ Starch/Bread, ½ Fruit, 1 Fat

NUTRIENTS PER SERVING:

Calories	180
% calories from fat	26
Total Fat	5 g
Saturated Fat	<1 g
Cholesterol	8 mg
Sodium	124 mg
Carbohydrate	30 g
Dietary Fiber	1 g
Protein	3 g
Calcium	45 mg
Iron	1 mg
Vitamin A	209 RE
Vitamin C	3 mg

Chocolate-Berry Cheesecake

1 cup chocolate wafer crumbs
1 container (12 ounces) fat
    free cream cheese
1 package (8 ounces) reduced
    fat cream cheese
⅔ cup sugar
½ cup cholesterol free egg
    substitute
3 tablespoons skim milk
1¼ teaspoons vanilla
1 cup mini semisweet
    chocolate chips
2 tablespoons raspberry all
    fruit spread
2½ cups fresh strawberries,
    stems removed, halved

1. Preheat oven to 350°F. Spray bottom of 9-inch springform pan with nonstick cooking spray.

2. Press chocolate wafer crumbs firmly onto side or bottom of prepared pan. Bake 10 minutes. Remove from oven; cool. *Reduce oven temperature to 325°F.*

3. Combine cheeses in large bowl with electric mixer. Beat at medium speed until well blended. Beat in sugar until well blended. Beat in egg substitute, milk and vanilla until well blended. Stir in mini chips with spoon. Pour batter into pan.

4. Bake 40 minutes or until center is set. Remove from oven; cool 10 minutes in pan on wire rack. Carefully loosen cheesecake from edge of pan. Cool completely.

5. Remove side of pan from cake. Blend fruit spread and 2 tablespoons water in medium bowl until smooth. Add strawberries; toss to coat. Arrange strawberries on top of cake. Refrigerate 1 hour before serving. Garnish with fresh mint, if desired.   *Makes 16 servings*

Dietary Exchanges per Serving:
1 Starch/Bread, ½ Lean Meat,
1 Fruit, 1 Fat

NUTRIENTS PER SERVING:

Calories	197
% calories from fat	29
Total Fat	7 g
Saturated Fat	2 g
Cholesterol	7 mg
Sodium	290 mg
Carbohydrate	29 g
Dietary Fiber	<1 g
Protein	7 g
Calcium	205 mg
Iron	1 mg
Vitamin A	172 RE
Vitamin C	13 mg

Peach & Blackberry Shortcakes

¾ **cup plain low fat yogurt, divided**
 5 **teaspoons sugar, divided**
 1 **tablespoon blackberry all fruit spread**
½ **cup coarsely chopped peeled peach**
½ **cup fresh or thawed frozen blackberries or raspberries**
½ **cup all-purpose flour**
¼ **teaspoon baking powder**
⅛ **teaspoon baking soda**
 2 **tablespoons reduced calorie margarine**
½ **teaspoon vanilla**

1. Place cheesecloth or coffee filter in large sieve or strainer. Spoon yogurt into sieve; place over large bowl. Refrigerate 20 minutes. Remove yogurt from sieve; discard liquid. Measure ¼ cup yogurt; blend remaining yogurt, 2 teaspoons sugar and fruit spread in small bowl. Refrigerate until ready to serve.

2. Meanwhile, combine peach, blackberries and ½ teaspoon sugar in medium bowl; set aside.

3. Preheat oven to 425°F.

4. Combine flour, baking powder, baking soda and remaining 2½ teaspoons sugar in small bowl. Cut in margarine with pastry blender until mixture resembles coarse crumbs. Combine reserved ¼ cup yogurt with vanilla. Stir into flour mixture just until dry ingredients are moistened. Shape dough into a ball.

5. Place dough on lightly floured surface. Knead dough gently 8 times. Divide dough in half. Roll out each half into 3-inch circle with lightly floured rolling pin. Place circles on ungreased baking sheet.

6. Bake 12 to 15 minutes or until lightly browned. Immediately remove from baking sheet. Cool shortcakes on wire rack 10 minutes or until cool enough to handle.

7. Cut shortcakes in half. Top bottom halves with fruit mixture, yogurt and remaining halves. Garnish with blackberries and mint, if desired. Serve immediately.

Makes 2 servings

Dietary Exchanges per Serving:
2½ Starch/Bread, ½ Milk, 1 Fruit, 1 Fat

NUTRIENTS PER SERVING:

Calories	327
% calories from fat	21
Total Fat	8 g
Saturated Fat	2 g
Cholesterol	5 mg
Sodium	311 mg
Carbohydrate	57 g
Dietary Fiber	4 g
Protein	8 g
Calcium	183 mg
Iron	2 mg
Vitamin A	176 RE
Vitamin C	11 mg

No-Guilt Chocolate Brownies

1 cup semisweet chocolate
    chips
¼ cup packed brown sugar
2 tablespoons granulated
    sugar
½ teaspoon baking powder
¼ teaspoon salt
½ cup cholesterol free egg
    substitute
1 jar (2½ ounces) first-stage
    baby food prunes
1 teaspoon vanilla
1 cup uncooked rolled oats
⅓ cup nonfat dry milk solids
¼ cup wheat germ
2 teaspoons powdered sugar

1. Preheat oven to 350°F. Spray
8-inch square baking pan with
nonstick cooking spray; set aside.
Melt chips in top of double boiler
over simmering water.

2. Combine brown and granulated
sugars, baking powder and salt in
large bowl with electric mixer. Add
egg substitute, prunes and vanilla.
Beat at medium speed until well
blended. Stir in oats, milk solids,
wheat germ and chocolate.

3. Pour batter into prepared pan.
Bake 30 minutes or until wooden
pick inserted in center comes out
clean. Cool completely. Cut into
2-inch squares. Dust with powdered
sugar before serving.

Makes 16 servings

Dietary Exchanges per Serving:
1 Starch/Bread, 1 Fat

NUTRIENTS PER SERVING:

Calories	124
% calories from fat	30
Total Fat	5 g
Saturated Fat	<1 g
Cholesterol	<1 mg
Sodium	65 mg
Carbohydrate	21 g
Dietary Fiber	<1 g
Protein	3 g
Calcium	33 mg
Iron	1 mg
Vitamin A	53 RE
Vitamin C	<1 mg

Blueberry Chiffon Cake

3 tablespoons reduced calorie
    margarine
¾ cup graham cracker crumbs
2 cups fresh or thawed frozen
    blueberries
2 envelopes unflavored gelatin
2 containers (8 ounces each)
    fat free cream cheese
1 container (8 ounces)
    Neufchâtel cheese
¾ cup sugar, divided
⅔ cup nonfat sour cream
½ cup lemon juice
1 tablespoon grated lemon
    peel
6 egg whites*

*Use only grade A clean, uncracked eggs.

1. Preheat oven to 350°F.

2. Melt margarine in small saucepan over medium heat. Stir in graham cracker crumbs. Press crumb mixture firmly onto bottom and 1 inch up side of 9-inch springform pan. Bake 10 minutes. Remove from oven. Cool 10 minutes. Arrange blueberries in a single layer on top of crust. Refrigerate until needed.

3. Place ½ cup cold water in small saucepan; sprinkle gelatin over water. Let stand 3 minutes to soften. Heat gelatin mixture over low heat until completely dissolved, stirring constantly.

4. Combine cheeses in large bowl with electric mixer. Beat at medium speed until well blended. Beat in ½ cup sugar until well blended. Beat in sour cream, lemon juice and lemon peel until well blended. Beat in gelatin mixture until well blended.

5. With clean, dry beaters, beat egg whites in medium bowl with electric mixer at medium speed until soft peaks form. Gradually add remaining ¼ cup sugar. Beat at high speed until stiff peaks form. Fold egg whites into cream cheese mixture. Gently spoon mixture into prepared crust. Cover with plastic wrap. Refrigerate 6 hours or until firm. *Makes 16 servings*

Dietary Exchanges per Serving:
½ Starch/Bread, 1 Lean Meat,
1 Fruit, ½ Fat

NUTRIENTS PER SERVING:

Calories	165
% calories from fat	28
Total Fat	5 g
Saturated Fat	2 g
Cholesterol	14 mg
Sodium	342 mg
Carbohydrate	20 g
Dietary Fiber	1 g
Protein	10 g
Calcium	229 mg
Iron	0 mg
Vitamin A	203 RE
Vitamin C	6 mg

Turtle Cheesecake

6 tablespoons reduced calorie
  margarine
1½ cups graham cracker
  crumbs
2 envelopes unflavored gelatin
2 containers (8 ounces each)
  fat free cream cheese
2 cups 1% low fat cottage
  cheese
1 cup sugar
1½ teaspoons vanilla
1 container (8 ounces)
  reduced fat nondairy
  whipped topping, thawed
¼ cup prepared fat free
  caramel topping
¼ cup prepared fat free hot
  fudge topping
¼ cup chopped pecans

1. Spray bottom and side of 9-inch springform pan with nonstick cooking spray. Preheat oven to 350°F. Melt margarine in small saucepan over medium heat. Stir in graham cracker crumbs. Press crumb mixture firmly onto side or bottom of prepared pan. Bake 10 minutes. Cool.

2. Place ½ cup cold water in small saucepan; sprinkle gelatin over water. Let stand 3 minutes to soften. Heat gelatin mixture over low heat until completely dissolved, stirring constantly.

3. Combine cream cheese, cottage cheese, sugar and vanilla in food processor or blender; process until smooth. Add gelatin mixture; process until well blended. Fold in whipped topping. Pour into prepared crust. Refrigerate 4 hours or until set.

4. Loosen cake from rim of pan. Remove side of pan from cake. Drizzle caramel and hot fudge toppings over cheesecake. Sprinkle pecans evenly over top of cake before serving.

Makes 16 servings

Dietary Exchanges per Serving:
2 Starch/Bread, ½ Lean Meat, 1 Fat

NUTRIENTS PER SERVING:

Calories	232
% calories from fat	26
Total Fat	7 g
Saturated Fat	1 g
Cholesterol	5 mg
Sodium	444 mg
Carbohydrate	32 g
Dietary Fiber	<1 g
Protein	10 g
Calcium	240 mg
Iron	1 mg
Vitamin A	164 RE
Vitamin C	1 mg

Fresh & Fruity Cobbler

Biscuit Topping (recipe
   follows)
5 teaspoons sugar, divided
1 teaspoon cornstarch
**½ cup fresh or thawed frozen
   blueberries**
½ cup peeled nectarine slices
**½ cup strawberries, stems
   removed, halved**

1. Preheat oven to 350°F. Prepare Biscuit Topping.

2. Blend ¼ cup water, 3 teaspoons sugar and cornstarch in small saucepan. Cook over medium heat 5 minutes or until mixture thickens, stirring constantly. Remove saucepan from heat; let stand 5 minutes.

3. Add blueberries, nectarine and strawberries to sugar mixture; toss to coat. Spoon fruit mixture into 2-cup casserole; sprinkle with remaining 2 teaspoons sugar. Drop tablespoonfuls topping around edge of casserole.

4. Bake 20 minutes or until topping is browned. Serve immediately.
Makes 2 servings

Biscuit Topping

⅓ cup all-purpose flour
1 tablespoon sugar
¼ teaspoon baking powder
⅛ teaspoon baking soda
**1 tablespoon plus 1 teaspoon
   reduced calorie margarine**
**3 tablespoons nonfat sour
   cream**
**2 teaspoons cholesterol free
   egg substitute**
¼ teaspoon vanilla

Combine flour, sugar, baking powder and baking soda in medium bowl. Cut in margarine with pastry blender until mixture resembles coarse crumbs. Blend remaining ingredients in small bowl. Stir into flour mixture just until dry ingredients are moistened.

Dietary Exchanges per Serving:
2 Starch/Bread, 1½ Fruit, ½ Fat

NUTRIENTS PER SERVING:

Calories	244
% calories from fat	16
Total Fat	4 g
Saturated Fat	1 g
Cholesterol	0 mg
Sodium	231 mg
Carbohydrate	48 g
Dietary Fiber	3 g
Protein	5 g
Calcium	50 mg
Iron	1 mg
Vitamin A	227 RE
Vitamin C	28 mg

Cheesy Cherry Turnovers

Butter-flavored nonstick cooking spray
1 package (8 ounces) reduced fat cream cheese, softened
1 cup 1% low fat cottage cheese
½ cup sugar, divided
1 teaspoon vanilla
1 can (16½ ounces) dark sweet pitted cherries, rinsed and drained
8 sheets frozen phyllo dough, thawed
1 cup whole wheat bread crumbs
1 teaspoon ground cinnamon

1. Preheat oven to 350°F. Spray baking sheet with cooking spray; set aside.

2. Combine cream cheese, cottage cheese, ¼ cup sugar and vanilla in medium bowl with electric mixer. Beat at medium speed until well blended. Stir in cherries.

3. Spray 1 phyllo dough sheet with cooking spray; fold sheet crosswise in half to form rectangle. Sprinkle with 2 tablespoons bread crumbs. Drop ⅓-cupful cheese mixture onto upper left corner of sheet. Fold left corner over mixture to form triangle. Continue folding triangle, right to left, until end of dough. Repeat with remaining ingredients. Place turnovers on prepared baking sheet. Combine remaining ¼ cup sugar with cinnamon. Sprinkle turnovers with sugar mixture.

4. Bake 12 to 15 minutes or until turnovers are crisp and golden brown. Serve warm or cold.
Makes 8 servings

Dietary Exchanges per Serving:
1 Starch/Bread, ½ Lean Meat, ½ Fruit, 1 Fat

NUTRIENTS PER SERVING:

Calories	170
% calories from fat	29
Total Fat	6 g
Saturated Fat	3 g
Cholesterol	11 mg
Sodium	314 mg
Carbohydrate	24 g
Dietary Fiber	1 g
Protein	8 g
Calcium	74 mg
Iron	1 mg
Vitamin A	170 RE
Vitamin C	1 mg

Triple Fruit Trifle

2 ripe pears, peeled, cored, coarsely chopped
2 ripe bananas, thinly sliced
1 tablespoon lemon juice
2 cups fresh or thawed frozen raspberries
¼ cup reduced calorie margarine
1 cup graham cracker crumbs
1 can (12 ounces) evaporated skim milk, divided
⅓ cup sugar
¼ cup cornstarch
⅓ cup cholesterol free egg substitute
2 tablespoons nonfat sour cream
1½ teaspoons vanilla
3 tablespoons apricot all fruit spread

1. Combine pears, bananas, lemon juice and raspberries in large bowl.

2. Melt margarine in small saucepan over medium heat. Stir in graham cracker crumbs until well blended. Remove saucepan from heat; set aside.

3. Blend ¼ cup milk, sugar and cornstarch in another small saucepan. Whisk in remaining milk. Bring to a boil over medium heat, stirring constantly. Boil 1 minute or until mixture thickens, stirring constantly. Reduce heat to medium-low.

4. Blend ⅓ cup hot milk mixture and egg substitute in small bowl. Add to milk mixture. Cook 2 minutes, stirring constantly. Remove saucepan from heat. Let stand 10 minutes, stirring frequently. Stir in sour cream and vanilla; blend well.

5. Spoon half of milk mixture into trifle dish or medium straight-sided glass serving bowl. Layer half of fruit mixture and ½ cup graham cracker crumb mixture over milk mixture. Repeat layers, ending with graham cracker crumb mixture. Blend fruit spread and 1 teaspoon water until smooth. Drizzle over trifle. Garnish with additional fresh fruit, if desired.

Makes 12 servings

Dietary Exchanges per Serving:
½ Starch/Bread, ½ Milk, 1½ Fruit, ½ Fat

NUTRIENTS PER SERVING:

Calories	181
% calories from fat	17
Total Fat	3 g
Saturated Fat	<1 g
Cholesterol	1 mg
Sodium	151 mg
Carbohydrate	34 g
Dietary Fiber	2 g
Protein	5 g
Calcium	124 mg
Iron	1 mg
Vitamin A	135 RE
Vitamin C	9 mg

Index

METRIC CONVERSION CHART

VOLUME MEASUREMENTS (dry)

⅛ teaspoon = 0.5 mL

¼ teaspoon = 1 mL

½ teaspoon = 2 mL

¾ teaspoon = 4 mL

1 teaspoon = 5 mL

1 tablespoon = 15 mL

2 tablespoons = 30 mL

¼ cup = 60 mL

⅓ cup = 75 mL

½ cup = 125 mL

⅔ cup = 150 mL

¾ cup = 175 mL

1 cup = 250 mL

2 cups = 1 pint = 500 mL

3 cups = 750 mL

4 cups = 1 quart = 1 L

VOLUME MEASUREMENTS (fluid)

1 fluid ounce (2 tablespoons) = 30 mL

4 fluid ounces (½ cup) = 125 mL

8 fluid ounces (1 cup) = 250 mL

12 fluid ounces (1½ cups) = 375 mL

16 fluid ounces (2 cups) = 500 mL

WEIGHTS (mass)

½ ounce = 15 g

1 ounce = 30 g

3 ounces = 90 g

4 ounces = 120 g

8 ounces = 225 g

10 ounces = 285 g

12 ounces = 360 g

16 ounces = 1 pound = 450 g

DIMENSIONS

1/16 inch = 2 mm

⅛ inch = 3 mm

¼ inch = 6 mm

½ inch = 1.5 cm

¾ inch = 2 cm

1 inch = 2.5 cm

OVEN TEMPERATURES

250°F = 120°C

275°F = 140°C

300°F = 150°C

325°F = 160°C

350°F = 180°C

375°F = 190°C

400°F = 200°C

425°F = 220°C

450°F = 230°C

BAKING PAN SIZES

Utensil	Size in Inches/ Quarts	Metric Volume	Size in Centimeters
Baking or Cake Pan (square or rectangular)	8×8×2	2 L	20×20×5
	9×9×2	2.5 L	23×23×5
	12×8×2	3 L	30×20×5
	13×9×2	3.5 L	33×23×5
Loaf Pan	8×4×3	1.5 L	20×10×7
	9×5×3	2 L	23×13×7
Round Layer Cake Pan	8×1½	1.2 L	20×4
	9×1½	1.5 L	23×4
Pie Plate	8×1¼	750 mL	20×3
	9×1¼	1 L	23×3
Baking Dish or Casserole	1 quart	1 L	—
	1½ quart	1.5 L	—
	2 quart	2 L	—